✵ INSIGHT COMPACT GUIDE

NORMANDY

Compact Guide: Normandy is the ultimate quick-reference guide to this delightful region of France. It tells you everything you need to know about the region's attractions, from its cathedrals to its châteaux, from its Calvados to its Camembert.

This is one of 133 Compact Guides, combining the interests and enthusiasms of two of the world's best-known information providers: Insight Guides, whose innovative titles have set the standard for visual travel guides since 1970, and Discovery Channel, the world's premier source of nonfiction television programming.

APA PUBLICATIONS
Part of the Langenscheidt Publishing Group

Star Attractions

An instant reference to some of Normandy's most popular tourist attractions to help you on your way.

Cathédrale Notre-Dame p19

Aître de St-Maclou p21

Etretat p29

Honfleur Vieux Port p46

Livarot p50

Calvados p53

Abbaye aux Hommes, Caen p59

Omaha Beach p63

Anse de Vauville p71

Bayeux p64

Mont St-Michel p73

NORMANDY

Introduction

Places

Culture

Leisure

Practical Information

Normandy – Land of Cheese and Calvados

Ramshackle cow sheds; Norman and Gothic churches and castle ruins sit harmoniously together; doves fly from dovecotes as strong as castle walls; thatched roofs are topped by irises; cattle rest under pink apple blossom; sheep graze on salty meadows at the edge of cliffs which drop abruptly into the sea; picture postcard half-timbered villages underneath the fluttering flags of Calvados and market stalls weighed down with heart-shaped cheeses. Who could ignore this corner of Europe?

Normandy appeals to the heart

It is easy to be drawn to a region which appeals so immediately to the heart. Where feelings and emotions run high, distances seem to matter little. Perhaps this is what makes it so easy to get close to Normandy. Over 600km (375 miles) of contrasting coastline includes beaches as flat and as safe as a bath-towel, alabaster chalk cliffs as high and as steep as the side of a skyscraper, wind-blown sand dunes, fishing villages and small ports with lobster pots piled high and luminous buoys beyond the quayside. Weather-beaten fishermen in berets sitting in the sun mending their nets; wooden boxes brim with scallops, whelks and oysters. The sea, here called *la Manche*, does not end at the beach in Normandy – it makes its mark on the whole region.

Between sailings

Its presence is felt on the thinly populated farmland of the Cotentin peninsula, surrounded on three sides by the English Channel, and equally on the monotonous Pays de Caux plateau. It breathes its salty breath through the wooded river valleys of the Bresle, Orne and Vire. Even the ancient cathedral city of Rouen, the region's biggest city some 110km (70 miles) from the coast, cannot escape the ceaseless tidal ebb and flow.

What makes Normandy so unique is not just its proximity to the sea. It is a region of fascinating contrasts. In the remotest regions amid fields of cauliflowers and beech hedges, suddenly there are fortresses, castles and ruined monasteries – all of which have played their part in 2,000 years of changing fortunes. It is a history shaped by Roman empire builders, pillaging Vikings, Norman dukes and French monarchs, by periods of pomp and splendour as well as by the dark days of plagues and wretched wars. Many a tiny village has found itself on the tourist itinerary thanks to its majestic Renaissance château, but visit the local *bar-tabac* afterwards and you will find yourself sharing the counter with the locals in their wellington boots who have called in on their way home from the fields.

Tension exists and it is not just between agriculture and art, yesterday and today. Fascinating paradoxes and contradictions are very much in evidence – and they are not always positive.

The beach at Cabourg

Position and topography

In a geographical sense, Normandy can justifiably be described as on the 'edge of Europe'. This region in the northwest of France extends from the densely populated Paris basin to the English Channel. It is bordered to the northeast by Picardy and to the southwest by Brittany. The 600km (375 mile) coastline is an unmistakable symbol of Normandy, characterised by the spectacular chalk cliffs at Etretat in the Pays de Caux, the inviting flat, sandy beaches in the *département* of Calvados and the fissured rocky coast and miles of sandy beaches on the Cotentin peninsula. With a surface area of almost 30,000sq km (11,600sq miles), Normandy is on a par with Belgium.

Normandy's geological sub-structure and topography are greatly varied. In Lower (Basse) Normandy, west of the imaginary Alençon-Valognes line, the region together with Brittany forms part of the granite Armorican Massif. Hills such as those in the Suisse Normande (Swiss Normandy) rise to just over 417m (1,300ft). Eastern or Upper (Haute) Normandy, on the other hand, is part of the wide Paris basin and consists of a flat plateau with sedimentary chalk and limestone reaching no more then 200m (650ft). The rivers Seine, Eure, Orne, Dives, Risle and Bresle flow through the region, with the Seine an important artery for river transport. On its banks lies the historic capital of Rouen and the city centre, largely rebuilt since 1945, is only a few metres away. Ships up to 10,000 tons use the large port complex.

A number of islands lie off the coast of the Cotentin peninsula, which extends north into the English Channel. The Channel Islands of Guernsey, Jersey and Alderney are of course British, the Iles Chausey, 17km (10 miles) from Granville, are French.

And what about the *bocage normand*? This term is used to describe the rural terrain to the east of Avranches. There, fields, meadows and orchards are often separated by ancient hedgerows, with narrow roads and tracks passing between. For centuries, these trees have protected the land from wind erosion and also provided the farmers with firewood. Over the centuries, the paths have worn down and the tips of the trees and bushes along many of the verges meet in the middle.

6

The chalk cliffs of Etretat

Flower market in Rouen

Climate

The mild, moist sea air provides the rainfall that gives the landscape its rich colour. The average temperature is 11–12°C (52–54°F) and the effects of the Gulf Stream ensure that, winter or summer, the mercury levels never register extremes and the exotic plants in the Parc Emmanuel-Liais in Cherbourg prove the point. On average there are fewer than 20 days of frost a year. In the interior, in the *bocage normand* for example, greater temperature fluctuations occur. Precipitation amounts to about 800mm (31in), most of which falls in the autumn and winter. The best time to visit Normandy is in July and August, but autumn can also be very pleasant as can May and June.

Nature and environment

Normandy is no more immune to change than other regions of France. Many barn doors have been bolted for good in the last few years and dairies have had to close because of low profits. Many of these have now been converted into *ferme-auberges*. Young people have been turning their backs on the country life for decades.

The deer are taking over

The 'green' image of Normandy has been tarnished, as the Seine has become the second most polluted river in France. On the coast, nuclear power stations and nuclear waste reprocessing plants are proof that the hi-tech age has caught up with the region. Nevertheless, there are some areas where great efforts have been made to preserve the natural environment. The Parc Naturel Régional de Brotonne extends along the Seine Valley from the mouth of the river to Le Trait. The western end of the region is known as the *Marais Vernier*, an unspoilt natural landscape in marshland close to the Seine estuary. Lying between St-Sauveur-le-Vicomte in the west and Treviers in the east, the Parc Régional des Marais du Cotentin et du Bessin extends over typical *bocage normand* as well as the marshland close to the Baie des Veys where the Vire, Sèves, Tortonne and Douve flow into the sea.

Population

Normandy has retained its rural character despite the three major conurbations of Rouen, Le Havre and Caen. The total population of the region is 3.5 million of which 1.76 million live in Haute Normandie and 1.40 million live in Basse

Three of a kind

Normandie, the remainder in Rouen. The term 'Norman' derives from the Viking 'Norsemen' who invaded the region in the 9th century and later took control when the Viking leader Rollo became the first Duke of Normandy.

Customs

Normandy is traditionally a region of farmers and fishermen, but the truth is that this part of France, like everywhere else, has had to keep up with the changes in society, and in the course of time, customs and traditions have been adapted or have simply died away. In some parts, however, the old ways have been retained and one such example is the weekly market, where farmers and local traders sell their produce directly to the community.

Pilgrimages to Normandy's many shrines have also continued. Mont St-Michel has long been a destination for pilgrims and, even during the Hundred Years' War, the feast of Archangel Michael was always celebrated on 29 September, drawing pilgrims who bought safe-conduct to the rocky island. Homage is now paid to St Michael on the Sunday nearest to that date.

Traditional head gear

Men, women and children still sometimes wear traditional costumes for certain festivals. On special occasions in the *département* of Calvados, women and girls can still be seen in long dresses and pointed hats. In some communities, hierarchical brotherhoods dedicated to a particular saint perform public ceremonies with banners, emblems and costumes. These organisations date from the 12th century when Brothers of Mercy attended to the funerals of plague victims. In Bernay, a brotherhood organises a procession every May.

Economy

The market at Rouen

The economy of Normandy cannot be described as a homogeneous unit, as many differences exist between the various *départements* or 'sub-regions'. Basse Normandie is oriented more to agriculture than Haute Normandie, where roughly 120,000 people or 24 percent of the working population are employed in industry (food, electrical goods, electronics and motor manufacturing), in line with the French average. In western Normandy, mainly the *département* of Manche, cattle and horse rearing and arable farming predominate. Dairy farming is important in the Pays d'Auge, where the world famous Camembert, Pont-l'Evêque and Livarot cheeses are made. Just under 20 percent of the working population are employed on the land in the *départements* of Manche and Orne, way above the national average of 6 per cent. A clearer picture of rural Normandy can be drawn from the fact that the region is responsible for 15 percent of the total French milk production. The Seine Valley and the Le Havre estuary are the major industrial regions. The port of Rouen benefits from the fact that it is only 110km (70 miles) from the English Channel and is accessible to deep-sea vessels. Le Havre is a major port for oil and oil-related imports and follows closely behind Marseille as France's busiest port. Chemical processing plays an important part in the local economy.

A prize specimen

Administration

Strictly speaking, Normandy, one of 22 French regions, is made up of the two sub-regions of Basse Normandie and Haute Normandie. The former consists of the *départements* of Calvados, Manche and Orne and the latter of Seine-Maritime and Eure. Since 1983, the joint region of Normandy has enjoyed decentralised responsibilities for the economy, education and training. At that time, all French regions acquired a degree of autonomy with a democratically elected council.

Norman tongue-twisters

Criquebec, Hambye, Houlgate, Ouistreham – Norman place-names which many French, let alone foreign visitors, have difficulty pronouncing. The reason is simple: these names are derived from Nordic, the language of the Viking invaders. From the beginning of the 10th century, when Normandy fell to Viking rule, the language of the Scandinavian settlers started to merge with the Latin-influenced French language. Some 1,000 years later, only place-names betray the Nordic roots of many of Normandy's early inhabitants. The *-fleur* ending, for example, meant 'flood' or 'fjord' and can be found in such names as Fiquefleur and Honfleur. The final syllable *-bec*, as in Orbec or Criquebec means stream and *-beuf*, as in Daubeuf and Lindebeuf, means house.

A windy day in Houlgate

Many other place-names have resulted from a combination of Scandinavian Christian names and the French ending *-ville*. This final syllable occurs in more than 30 percent of all place-names, well above the average for the whole of France. Besneville and Bierville, for example, are derived from Björn, Rauville and Rouville from Hrolf, Veauville and Vauville from Valr and Touffrainville from Thorfrod.

9

One difficult name to pronounce is Ouistreham, a coastal town on the Côte de Nacre. Etymologists have concluded that *Ouistre* almost certainly comes from the Anglo-Saxon word *ouster* meaning east, while *ham* is a Germanic suffix for a small settlement or farmhouse. In French the word *hameau* means a small village or hamlet.

Half-timbered house in Honfleur

Historical Highlights

58–51 BC Roman troops under Julius Caesar conquer the resident celtic tribes in the northwest of what is now France, and establish their regional capital at Rotomagus (Rouen).

52 BC The Romans found the towns of Harfleur and Lisieux.

260 St Mellon is first bishop of Rouen.

486 Normandy conquered by Frankish Merovingian empire under King Clovis.

7th century The first monasteries established in Jumièges and Fontanelle in the Seine Valley.

708 Abbey of Mont St-Michel founded.

820 The first Viking raids up the Seine Valley.

841 Vikings invade Normandy, plundering the abbey at Jumièges, and destroying Rouen.

911 Rollo, the Viking leader, and the French king, Charles le Simple, sign the Treaty of St-Clair-sur-Epte to found the Duchy of Normandy.

933 Accession of William Longsword; monastery rebuilding begins.

1027 Birth of William the Conqueror. By 1047, he has succeeded in overcoming his political rivals.

1066 William defeats Harold at the Battle of Hastings and becomes king of England.

1087 Death of William the Conqueror in Rouen and is buried in the Abbaye aux Hommes in Caen.

1180–1223 Philippe-Auguste, king of France, reinforces castles in Normandy.

1195 Richard Lionheart, king of England, builds Château Gaillard.

1204 Château Gaillard captured by Philippe-Auguste, who goes on to conquer all Normandy except for the Isles Normandes (Channel Islands) and the duchy is united with the French crown.

1315 Normandy awarded provincial status.

1337 The English king Edward III revives his claim to the French throne, marking the beginning of the Hundred Years' War.

1346 English victorious at the Battle of Crécy.

1415 Henry V of England arrives at Honfleur and takes all Normandy.

1431 Accused of sorcery and heresy, Joan of Arc is burned at the stake in Rouen.

1437 Caen University is founded.

1453 All of France, except for Calais, is back in French hands.

1469 The French monarchy gives up the title to the duchy of Normandy.

1517 Le Havre founded by François I.

1572 The St Batholomew's Day Massacre of Protestant Hugenots; 500 killed in Rouen.

1598 The Edict of Nantes grants the Huguenots religious and civil liberties.

1630–36 Serious plague epidemic strikes Normandy.

1685 Louis XIV, the Sun King, revokes the Edict of Nantes and begins the persecution of the Huguenots.

1692 Fleet sets sail from La Hougue to restore James II to the English throne, and is disastrously defeated.

1756–63 Seven Years' War with England.

1789–92 The French Revolution leads to the First Republic. Monasteries abandoned and destroyed. Normandy ceases to exist as a province.

1804–14 First Empire is established under Napoleon Bonaparte.

1830 Charles X goes into exile in Cherbourg.

1843 Completion of railway line from Paris to Rouen.

1848 Rioting in Rouen. King Louis-Philippe leaves Honfleur for exile in Britain.

1856 *Madame Bovary* by Gustave Flaubert published, outraging the citizens of Rouen.

1850 Guy de Maupassant, the great Norman writer, is born near Fécamp.

1870–1 Upper Normandy occupied during Franco-Prussian war.

1914–18 World War I.

1920 Joan of Arc canonised and becomes patron saint of France.

1932 The ocean liner *Normandie* breaks transatlantic records.

1939–45 World War II.

1940 France capitulates to Germany and all of France is occupied. Towns and cities in Haute Normandie ravaged by fire.

1942 Canadian attempt to create a bridgehead in Dieppe fails with huge loss of life.

1944 'Operation Overlord' begins at daybreak on 6 June (D-Day). Allied forces land at several locations along the Normandy coast. Bitter fighting culminates in the Falaise Pocket, 22 August.

1957 France becomes a founder member of the European Economic Community.

1976 A deep-sea harbour for supertankers constructed at Cap d'Antifer.

1982 The Oscar Niemeyer Cultural Centre opened in Le Havre.

1994 Completion of the Pont de Normandie Seine crossing between Le Havre and Honfleur. 50th anniversary of the D-Day landings.

2003 Juno Beach Museum and Information Centre, Courseulles-sur-Mer opens on 6 June. It is a memorial and tribute to Canadian forces who landed on Juno Beach on D-Day.

2004 60th D-Day anniversary.

The Hundred Years' War

Dynastic feuds have frequently wreaked death and destruction upon innocent subjects, but for a marriage to precipitate a war between two nations which lasted for over a hundred years, was an exceptional case even by European standards. The momentous marriage bond was struck in 1152 at the church of St-Pierre in Lisieux when Henry II, the Plantagenet duke of Normandy, wed Eleanor of Aquitaine. Two years later, Henry was crowned king of England. As a consequence, not just England and Normandy, but also large parts of western France, such as Aquitaine, Anjou, Gascony and Brittany, were united under one throne. The Angevin Empire remained intact until Phillip II (1180–1223) captured parts of the empire, including Normandy (1204), for France.

Almost 200 years after the Lisieux marriage, the English king Edward III set about re-uniting the English and French crowns under his rule. With the death of Charles IV in 1328, the Capetian dynasty ended. As nephew of the former French king, Edward made claims on the French throne, thereby precipitating the Hundred Years' War (1337–1453). Of those 116 years, however, only 53 were in fact years of war, the rest were relatively peaceful. From what was initially a feudal power struggle among the Capetian pretenders, a bitter war between England and France developed and Normandy was the main battleground.

No other people suffered as much as a result of this feud between London and Paris. About one third of the total population died during those 116 years. Civilians suffered badly at the hands of the English who for the first time deployed cannons in the Battle of Crécy (1346). As well as the immediate effects of the war, the rural population suffered from the devastation of their land and from marauding brigands. Soon afterwards, a plague originating in Asia struck Europe, developing into one of the worst catastrophes ever to affect the western world.

Under the leadership of Joan of Arc, the Maid of Orléans, French troops won significant victories over the English who were eventually expelled. When the Hundred Years' War came to an end in 1453, political and social life had undergone dramatic changes. The English threat had, in fact, united the French people into one nation. Furthermore, a modern system of taxation, a professional army and an elementary civil service had been created – the basic elements for the absolutist state, which was later to be realised.

Place du Vieux-Marché

Route 1

Rouen: a peep-hole into the Middle Ages

As the sun sets over the Atlantic, the Middle Ages appears to return to Rouen's old town centre of cobbled streets and gabled half-timbered houses. Doorways and shadowy corners look even darker in the dim light of the wrought-iron lanterns and when the clock tower chimes, the heart of the town could easily be mistaken for the film set of *The Three Musketeers* – but with the difference that, in Normandy's principal city, the half-timbered houses with their centuries-old façades, the Gothic church with its ornate towers and the solid Renaissance palace are not just a backdrop, but the stuff of history, architectural gems which have survived both dreadful misfortune and artistic and economic prosperity.

Rouen's centre of narrow alleys and weathered façades, its crumbling plaster and soaring Gothic towers will cap-

16

tivate you as soon as you cross from the modern ring road lined by functional but dull office blocks to the old town, a place that rouses heart and soul.

From the surrounding hillsides with their famous viewpoints such as the Basilique de Bonsecours or the suburb of Canteleu, the sea of roofs and towers could be any French city. But once immersed in the old heart of this Norman metropolis, then history overtakes you as if the Middle Ages had never ended.

Baguettes are best eaten fresh

Rouen is linked by rail to most major French cities. About 20 trains per day run between Rouen and Paris and the 139-km (86-mile) journey takes about 75 minutes. A scheduled bus service connects Rouen with most tourist destinations in the region.

History

The most famous event in the history of Rouen is the burning of Joan of Arc at the stake in 1431, but the city's history extends much further back than that – to before the Christian era. With its sand-banks and islands, this crossing-point on the Seine was settled by Gauls of the Veliocasse tribe. The settlement was named 'Rotomagus' by Julius Caesar's army who conquered it around 58–51BC. The town developed quickly and in 260 Bishop Mellon chose it as his first seat. In subsequent centuries the town continued to grow until the arrival of the Vikings in 841 brought its period of prosperity to an end. By the beginning of the 10th century, however, a community had been re-established there. Under the Treaty of St-Clair-sur-Epte (911), which created the Duchy of Normandy, Rollo, the Viking leader, chose Rouen as his capital and set about building a port.

The French king Phillip II conquered Normandy in 1204 and united it with France, but it was not until 1450, after the Hundred Years' War when the English were finally expelled, that Rouen and the rest of Normandy became a part of France again.

Rouen's golden age followed, lasting until the beginning of the Wars of Religion in 1562. The church of St-Maclou was built then in Flamboyant style as well as the cathedral's Tour de Beurre (Butter Tower). Under the influence of Rouen's Archbishop Georges I d'Amboise, late Gothic was succeeded by Italian Renaissance, a style which marked many of the town's secular buildings. A number of faience factories and weaving mills were built in the town, helping to create a busy and important industrial centre, and at the same time Rouen was emerging as a major port. Maritime travel was just starting to increase contact between trading nations at opposite ends of the globe. However, the Wars of Religion (1562–98)

17

Cobbled alleys

The cathedral's Butter Tower

and the Thirty Years' War (1618–48) had an adverse effect on Rouen's prosperity. The Revocation of the Edict of Nantes in 1685, which resulted in the Huguenots, who were mainly merchants and traders fleeing abroad, added to the town's decline. But with the invention in the 18th century of new machines for the textile industry and new materials, the town's fortunes were reversed. In 1843 the railway network was extended to include Rouen and the port complex was enlarged.

German troops occupied Haute Normandie during the Franco-Prussian War (1870–71), but it was World War II which inflicted most damage on Rouen. Almost the whole of the old town, as well as large parts of the industrial quarter, was destroyed. After the reconstruction and restoration of large parts of the old centre and the development of new housing estates and office blocks such as the *Cité Administrative* on the other side of the river, Rouen's population has grown to 400,000 and it is now the largest and most important industrial city in Normandy.

The Old Town

The Old Town, Rouen's window on to the past, lies on the north bank of the Seine. It is undoubtedly best to visit it on foot and in any case, car parking space is at a premium. Allow about 3 hours for this journey back into the Middle Ages. Add more time for visiting museums.

Display of oysters at the Place du Vieux-Marché

The ★ **Place du Vieux-Marché ❶**. A 20-m (65-ft) cross marks the spot where in 1431 Joan of Arc was burnt at the stake. Now the patron saint of France, she is remembered in the adjacent futuristic church, which dates from 1979. The superb 16th-century stained glass windows were retrieved from the St-Vincent church, which was destroyed in 1944.

The nearby market hall is used by farmers from the outlying rural areas to sell their cheese and also their bread, often baked in wood-fired ovens. In the autumn, freshly pressed cider in large glass bottles will be on sale too.

Musée Jeanne d'Arc

A row of ancient half-timbered buildings border the south side of the square. Sample the taste of Normandy in one of the traditional restaurants here and pay a quick visit to the **Musée Jeanne d'Arc** (open daily but closed Monday in winter) with its waxwork models. The birthplace of the great French dramatist, Pierre Corneille (1606–84), is now the ★ **Maison Natale de Corneille** (4 rue de la Pie, tel: 02 35 71 63 92; open daily except Tuesday and Wednesday morning 10am–noon, 2–6pm) ❷. His study contains chairs, armchairs and other 17th-century furniture.

The ★ **Rue du Gros-Horloge** starts at the southeast corner of the Place du Vieux-Marché. This busy, cobbled street contains modern shops, most of which have been rebuilt since World War II, but they are in stark contrast to the many half-timbered buildings in the town centre.

Musée Flaubert et d'Histoire de la Médecine (51 rue de Lecat, tel: 02 35 15 59 95; open Wednesday to Saturday, 10am–noon, 2–6pm, Tuesday 10am–6pm). Located in the Hôtel-Dieu where Gustave Flaubert was born and where his father was a surgeon. The museum has memorabilia of the great writer as well as exhibits of 19th century hospital instruments and a garden of medicinal plants.

The ★★ **Gros Horloge** ❸ is a large single-handed clock which has become one of Rouen's principal tourist attractions especially since restoration when it was reopened in Spring 2003. The golden clock-face which resembles a flaming sun was installed in the arch over the street in 1527. The adjoining **beffroi**, or bell-tower, once played an important part in a dispute between the people and the state. In 1382, when another tax increase was announced, a group of angry citizens organised a revolt by ringing both bells in the tower. King Charles VI's response was simply to demolish the upper part of the tower, thereby depriving the townsfolk of an important weapon.

Nowhere in the network of alleys and lanes is the medieval architecture quite so striking as on the **Place de la Cathédrale**. This extensive square is dominated by the impressive west facade of the ★★★ **Cathédrale Notre-Dame** ❹ (open daily 8am–7pm, Sunday till 6pm), one of the finest examples of French Gothic. Started in the 12th century, it was not finished until 1530. The eye is automatically drawn to the rose window at the centre of the west front and then the multitude of ornate figures. The 82-m (268-ft) **Tour St-Romain** on the left dates from the 12th century, while on the right the late Gothic **Tour de Beurre** with 56 bells was built between 1485 and 1507. The term 'butter tower' refers to a practice adopted during the Middle Ages. During Lent, wealthy citizens who

Rue du Gros-Horloge and detail of the clock

19

Cathédrale Notre-Dame

Tomb of William Longsword

Escalier de la Librairie

Rue Malpalu

did not wish to fast bought a dispensation. The amount that the church collected was known as 'butter money' and this money is said to have been used to build the tower.

An almost mystical feel pervades the dark interior, often emphasised by a rich smell of incense, as the huge walls surrounding the 135-m (442-ft) long and 28-m (91-ft) high nave keep at bay the city's hustle and bustle. The choir and crypt are certainly the oldest parts of the building, which was constructed on the remains of a Roman temple. The ambulatory holds the recumbent figures of three famous Normans, each one having made his mark on the history of the region. In the first tomb rests Rollo, whose oath sealed the Treaty of Clair-sur-Epte in AD911. In the second tomb lies his son Guillaume Longue-Epée (William Longsword), who enlarged the duchy of Normandy to the Cotentin peninsula and around Avranches. The third tomb contains Richard I, the Lionheart, who died on 6 April, 1199 from blood poisoning after he was struck by an arrow in battle. The tombs of the cardinals of Amboise can be found in the Lady Chapel, where Georges I d'Amboise and II – uncle and nephew – are shown kneeling. This early Renaissance tomb, which was created between 1515 and 1525, is one of the finest sculptures in the cathedral.

Two portals lead off the transept. The richly ornamented **Portail de la Calende** in the southern arm portrays the martyrs and the baptism of Jesus. The **Portail des Libraires** (Booksellers' Doorway) at the north side is more striking with a sculpture of the Last Judgement in the tympanum. Before leaving the cathedral through this doorway, take a quick look at the finely carved **Escalier de la Librairie** (Booksellers' Staircase).

The late Gothic Flamboyant style can be found on many of the sacred buildings in the town, including the fine example of ★★ **St-Maclou** ❺ (open Monday to Saturday 10am–noon, 2–6pm, Sunday 3–5.30pm). The most remarkable feature about this church is that it was built in late Gothic Flamboyant style between 1437 and 1517, a period when Renaissance style was already well established.

Rue Malpalu and **Rue Damiette** near St-Maclou give visitors the best impression of what the town centre would have looked like in the Middle Ages. The best half-timbered houses in Rouen are said to be in ★ **Rue Martainville**, which runs along the northern side of the church. An entrance by 184–186 Rue Martainville leads to ★★ **Aître de St-Maclou** ❻ (open daily 8am–8pm), a rectangular inner courtyard. During the plagues of the 16th century this courtyard was used as a mortuary. Between 1630 and 1636, about 20 percent of Rouen's population perished from the Black Death. The carvings on the two-storey gallery, now used by students from the **Ecole des**

Beaux-Arts (Academy of Fine Art), display macabre motifs of skulls, crossbones and various gravediggers' tools.

Carved skull in the Aître de St-Maclou

The church of ★★ **St-Ouen ❼** (open Wednesday to Monday 10am–12.30pm, 2–6pm in summer; Wednesday, Saturday and Sunday 10am–12.30pm, 2–4.30pm in winter) stands in the small park adjoining the Town Hall (**Hôtel de Ville**). An abbey is said to have stood here around AD750. The lawn nearby marks the place where Joan of Arc was sentenced to death. The best view of this Gothic church is from the south or east side of the old monastery garden The 82m (268ft) tower has become a symbol of the region. Topped with a ducal coronet it is known today as 'the Crown of Normandy'.

With a total of five museums, **Place St-Godard**, named after the church of ★ **St-Godard ❽**, is regarded as Rouen's cultural centre. The ★★ **Musée des Beaux-Arts ❾** (Esplanade Marcel-Duchamp, tel: 02 35 71 28 40; open Wednesday to Sunday 10am–6pm, Monday 4pm for guided tour of permanent collections) is perhaps the best known. It mainly houses works by Norman artists. A part of the museum is dedicated to Théodore Géricault (1791–1824), who was born in Rouen and spent his childhood there. French Impressionism is also well represented since some celebrated painters such as Claude Monet, Auguste Renoir and Alfred Sisley lived and worked in the region. The **Musée de la Céramique ❿** (1 rue Faucon, tel: 02 35 07 31 74; open Wednesday to Monday 10am–1pm, 2–6pm) is also interesting. By 1550, the production of quality pottery was making an important contribution to Rouen's prosperity and, around 1644, a design involving blue decorative work on a white background was adopted in the local factories.

Musée des Beaux-Arts

The **Tour Jeanne d'Arc ⓫** (open Monday to Saturday 10am–12.30pm, 2–6pm, Sunday 2–6.30pm, till 5.30pm in winter) in Rue du Donjon holds reminders of Rouen's darker hours. Joan of Arc was threatened with torture here but imprisoned in another tower which no longer exists.

The ★★ **Palais de Justice ⓬** (open Thursday to Monday 10am–6pm, Wednesday 2–6pm) in Place Maréchal-Foch on the other hand represents a time of grandeur and wealth. Badly damaged during World War II, it has been fully restored. During renovation in 1976 the remains of a synagogue dating back to around 1100 were unearthed. The so-called 'Monument Juif' (Jewish Monument) is the oldest in France.

Palais de Justice

While in Rouen, visitors should ask in the Syndicat d'Initiative for information on sightseeing tours to the monasteries in the Seine Valley (*see page 22*). The tourist office will also have details of boat trips around the port.

Abbaye St-Georges-de-Boscherville

BRITAIN

Paris

FRANCE

Route 2

Route des Abbayes:
Rouen – Le Havre (110km/68 miles)

The Seine makes its way to the Atlantic coast alongside chalk cliffs, wooded hillsides and country villages. In pre-Christian times the river was an important artery and it remains so. The Romans settled in farmsteads along its banks and founded important towns such as Juliobona, modern Lillebonne *(see page 24)*. With the advent of Christianity, monks also started to build their monasteries close to the river and in the centuries that followed these contributed greatly to the economic prosperity and cultural richness of the region. The modern Route des Abbayes runs more or less parallel to the river and although many of the abbeys are in a poor state, their splendour bears witness to a distinguished era.

The railway line from Rouen to Le Havre and Fécamp passes through Yvetot, 10km (6 miles) north of Caudebec-en-Caux *(see page 24)*. Buses between Rouen and Le Havre pass through Caudebec-en-Caux, as well as Boscherville, Jumièges, St-Wandrille, Villequier and Bolbec.

A family outing

Sights

Just beyond the outskirts of Rouen, the Route des Abbayes passes through the Forêt de Roumare, before the ★ **Abbaye St-Georges-de-Boscherville** (open daily 1 April to 31 October 9am–6.30pm; 1 November to 31 March 2–5pm; closed Christmas Day and New Year's Day) in the small village of St-Martin-de-Boscherville 10km (6 miles) northwest of Rouen. Archaeologists have uncovered evidence that the site had previously been used as a heathen temple, but it was in the middle of the 11th century that Raoul de Tancarville, William the Conqueror's chamberlain, decided to build a monastery here and from 1114 it was run by Benedictine monks. The abbey church represents one of the purest examples of Romanesque architecture. Recent renovation has restored the gleaming white limestone and the level of craftsmanship visible on the statue columns is unique to Normandy.

Abbaye de Jumièges

Among orchards and meadows lies one of the province's finest monuments, the ★★★ **Abbaye de Jumièges** (open daily 15 April to 15 September 9.30am–7pm; 16 September to 14 April 9.30am–1pm, 2.30–5.30pm; closed public holidays; Seasonal illuminated night visits). The huge west front of the former **Notre-Dame** abbey church is relatively well preserved. Built between 1040 and 1067 it was consecrated by William the Conqueror, but in the 12th and 13th centuries it underwent a number of alterations which reflected the contemporary architectural trends still visible in the shape of the imposing twin towers.

Tower detail, Jumièges

23

St Philibert, who lived around 654, is said to be the founder of the monastery. Plundered by the Vikings in 841, it was abandoned until 940 and over the next 70 years, the whole complex was rebuilt to its original dimensions. Furthermore, the abbey succeeded in advancing its economic and political influence in the region. As a visible proof of its increasing power, the abbey church was extended by the addition of two new naves and the **Eglise St-Pierre** was also enlarged. During the monastery's heyday, over 1,000 monks and 1,500 lay brethren lived in the complex which also owned extensive estates in the vicinity. The two Jumièges churches are linked by the pre-Romanesque **Passage Charles VI**.

Before the Hundred Years' War, indeed even before the beginning of the Wars of Religion in 1562, the decline of the abbey had started and it was not until the first half of the last century that historians started to assess the cultural and political impact of Jumièges.

The foundation stone for the **Abbaye Notre-Dame-de-Fontennelle** in **Wandrille-Rançon** (pop. 1,500) was laid even earlier than that of Jumièges. Around AD629 Count Wandrille renounced his position at the court of King Dagobert. He later returned to the Fontanelle Valley and founded ★ **St-Wandrille Abbey** which was to flourish until the Wars of Religion. It fell into disuse during the Revolution but in 1931 Benedictine monks returned. Guided tours (Monday to Saturday 3 and 4pm, Sunday 11.30am, 3 and 4pm) include the inner courtyard which is entered from the **Porte de Jarente**, built in the 18th century by the bishop of Orléans. Apart from a transept and the cloister gallery, very little of the once fine Gothic abbey remains.

St-Wandrille Abbey

Caudebec-en-Caux (pop. 2,500) on the right bank of the Seine is the ideal place to stop for a short break. Of architectural interest is the late Gothic church of ★ **Notre-Dame** with its tower in the form of a stone tiara. In its shadow every Saturday, farmers and traders exercise their 600-year right to sell their produce in the **Place du Marché**. Much of the town was destroyed by fire in 1940, but the 13th-century Maison des Templiers survived and is now used as a local history museum (open April to June Saturday and Sunday 2–6pm; July to September Wednesday to Monday 2–6pm.

Victor Hugo caricature and museum exhibit

Victor Hugo is responsible for putting **Villequier** (pop. 900) on the tourist trail. The estate of the Vacquerie family lies on the banks of the Seine and the son married Hugo's daughter, Léopoldine. During one of their many visits, a boat trip on the Seine ended in tragedy and they both drowned. For the author the death of his daughter was a terrible blow and it became a recurring theme in his subsequent writing. The **Musée Victor-Hugo** (tel: 02 35 56 78 31; open 10am–12.30pm, 2–6pm, closed Tuesday and Sunday morning) is now installed in the Vacqueries' house and contains paintings, photos, drawings and other memorabilia. The tombs of Hugo's wife and members of the Vacquerie family can be seen in the church cemetery.

Lillebonne (pop. 10,000) was an important inland harbour for the Romans and William the Conqueror, recognising its strategic position, built a castle here, but only the 34-m (111-ft) round tower has survived. Nearby the **Musée des Arts et Traditions Populaires** (7 Rue Victor Hugo) houses many 18th- and 19th-century exhibits of historical interest. The museum (or the café in the Hôtel de Ville) can also provide the key to Lillebonne's best known sight, a ★ **Roman amphitheatre**, dating from the early years of the Roman occupation.

Château Filières, with its gleaming white facade of Caen stone, lies to the west of Bolbec near the village of

Musée du Prieuré

Gommerville. Only the left wing of the original 16th-century structure remains. The rest was restored in the 18th century and is now furnished with antiques.

The **Musée du Prieuré** is to be found in **Harfleur** on the eastern edge of Le Havre and was used in the Middle Ages as a hospital for sick seamen.

The **Prieuré de Graville**, also on the eastern side of Le Havre, is the last stop on the Route des Abbayes. Situated in rue Elysée-Reclus, the pillars in the nave of the chapel are part of the original Romanesque priory. The former monastery building now houses the **Musée du Prieuré de Graville**, with some fascinating examples of folk art. There is also an interesting collection of over 200 model houses, displaying in miniature a wide range of Norman architectural styles.

Route 3

Le Havre:
Boulevard Albert I

Le Havre: The Norman phoenix

No town in Normandy suffered during World War II as much as Le Havre. Apart from one or two exceptions, the town centre had to be almost completely rebuilt after 1945 and Le Havre rose phoenix-like from the ashes to acquire a new face and a new identity.

St Joseph's church

Direct trains link Le Havre to Paris via Rouen. Buses serve Fécamp via Etretat and Honfleur or Caen via Pont-Audemer.

History

1945 was not the first time that Le Havre evolved from a town planner's drawing board. In 1517, François I (1515–49) ordered the construction of a port to replace Harfleur which was silting up. At the beginning of the Wars of Religion the devoutly Protestant town passed to the English after the Treaty of Hampton Court, but within barely a year it was returned to France. After the government of Henri IV made attempts to modernise the port facilities, it was left to the governor of Le Havre, Cardinal Richelieu, to complete the expansion. Jean Baptiste Colbert, Louis XIV's minister of finance, culture and the navy, was responsible not only for enlarging France's colonial empire but also for developing overseas trade from Le Havre, especially with the East Indies. Disputes with England led to a bombardment in February 1694 and further attacks in July 1759 caused considerable damage. However, economic prosperity returned later that century with the independence of the American colonies in 1776, as European trade with the New World shifted from English ports to French ports. Later, Le Havre lost its impor-

Contemplating the past

tant role as a naval base to Cherbourg, but by the middle of the 19th century the town's population of 58,000 was profiting greatly from transatlantic passenger transport and trade.

During World War I Le Havre was an important supply base for the Allied troops stationed in northern France and the Belgian government in exile sought refuge there. After the war, luxury passenger ships sailed from Le Havre to New York and the French Caribbean islands, and the town once again returned to prominence as a major transatlantic passenger terminal.

During World War II, however, Allied bombing brought destruction on a massive scale. 80,000 inhabitants lost their homes, 10,000 buildings were destroyed and as very little of the old town remained, almost total reconstruction started in 1946 under the direction of the French architect Auguste Perret.

LE HAVRE

0   300 m

Sights

At the heart of the new town lies the **Place de l'Hôtel de Ville** . Geometrical designs characterise this huge square, one of the largest in Europe. The plain **Hôtel de Ville** houses the city's administrative offices, as well as the **Office de Tourisme**.

Villa Maritime, Boulevard Albert I

Neglected by the local people for many years, Le Havre's **beach** ❷ has undergone a facelift. The section of coast which runs parallel to **Boulevard Albert I** has been converted into a leisure area with a stream winding its way through the middle. Sports facilities, snack bars, restaurants and shops line the new promenade which is proving popular with the local people and also visitors.

Similarly, the municipal marina or **Port de Plaisance** ❸ has become a favourite destination for a stroll on summer evenings. Overlooking the marina stands the plain concrete tower of **Eglise St-Joseph** ❹ (open daily). Topped by an octagonal bell tower (109m/357ft), this 1950s church designed by Auguste Perret stands out on the city skyline. The bare walls of this striking monument are broken up by colourful, glass tiles which allow sufficient diffused daylight to enter the interior.

Eglise St-Joseph, interior

Only a few yards from the marina is the **Musée des Beaux-Arts André Malraux** ❺ (2 Boulevard Clémenceau, tel: 02 35 19 62 62; Wednesday to Monday 11am–6pm, Saturday and Sunday till 7pm). Another modern construction of glass, aluminium and steel, it was built in 1961 and has since become an important cultural centre. In front of the museum is a sculpture by HG Adam which dates from the same year. This huge concrete structure is known locally as the 'Eye', enhancing the centre's reputation as an top-class art museum – a reputation which now extends throughout France and beyond.

Most of the exhibits were formerly displayed in a museum which was destroyed in the last war. They represent a cross-section of European art from the last 300 years with many works by French, Flemish and Dutch painters. However, artists who painted in Normandy, such as Eugène Boudin, Raoul Dufy, Claude Monet, Camille Pissarro, and Jean Dubuffet are given prominence.

Notre-Dame detail

Terminal de Grande-Bretagne ❻ is the destination for ferries arriving from England and is situated only a few yards from the town centre. The harbour attracts considerable interest from locals and visitors alike.

Those in search of peace and quiet, however, are more likely to find it in the **Cathédrale Notre-Dame** ❼ (open daily). Completion was delayed by the Wars of Religion in the second half of the 16th century. The west front was finished in 1630 and the building then survived until World War II when it was badly damaged in bombing raids. The church organ with beautifully carved wooden sections

Bassin du Roi
Quartier St-François

The Passerelle

dates from 1637. It was not spared by the bombs either, but has been restored; *le Grand Orgue* was finally reinstalled in 1980.

A building nearby which suffered a similar fate is the **Musée d'Histoire Naturelle ❽** (tel: 02 35 41 37 28). The original museum was housed in Le Havre's Palais de Justice, which had to be completely rebuilt. Apart from the architectural loss many fine ornithological, mineralogical and zoological exhibits could not be replaced.

Just east of the museum lie the **Bassin du Roi** and the **Bassin du Commerce**, two inner docks which are linked to the outer harbour. These two docks form two sides of Le Havre's oldest district, the **Quartier St-François**. A glance at the map will show that it is almost an island, linked to the rest of the town with bridges. Formerly the site of the fish market, it too has yielded to recent modernisation. The **Musée de l'Ancien Havre** (1 rue Jérôme-Bellarmato, tel: 02 35 42 27 90; open Wednesday to Sunday 10am–noon, 2–6pm) houses maps, plans and models which show clearly how Le Havre looked in the 19th century. The **Musée Maritime et Portuaire** (Centre Culturel Maritime, Hangar 22, quai de Norvège) is not just for amateur sailors with an interest in boats and boatbuilding, but for anyone interested in an era when dockworkers unloaded sacks of coffee from Brazil, cotton from India and spices from the Far East.

Looking like a concrete archer's bow supported by steel cables, the **Passerelle ❾**, a footbridge, crosses the Bassin du Commerce. It serves as both a short cut for pedestrians into the town centre and a viewpoint over the central **Place Niemeyer**. Here stands the principal symbol of Le Havre's rebirth, the ultramodern **Maison de la Culture du Havre ❿**. Opened in 1982, it was designed by the celebrated Brazilian architect Oscar Niemeyer. The complex consists of two asymmetrical buildings. The larger one houses a theatre, cinema and exhibition centre and is known to locals as *le Grand Volcan* (the big volcano), although it has been compared to the cooling tower of a nuclear power station or an upturned yoghurt pot. *Le Petit Volcan* is on a smaller scale and facilities here include an auditorium and conference rooms.

The sea still provides Le Havre with its prosperity. It is France's premier container port. The **Ecluse François I**, a huge lock 401m (1,315ft) long, 67m (219ft) wide and 24m (78ft) deep is one of the biggest locks in the world and can 'raise' vessels of up to 250,000 tons.

In the suburb of Graville, a little further out of the town centre, lies the **Abbaye de Graville** (Rue de l'Abbaye), where the Romanesque church of Ste-Honorine, one of the oldest sacred buildings in the Le Havre area, can be seen (*see page 24*).

Route 4

The Alabaster Coast:
Le Havre – Le Tréport (150km/93 miles)

The most spectacular section of the whole Normandy coast is the **Côte d'Albâtre** or Alabaster Coast. It forms the shore-line between Le Havre and Le Tréport in the Seine-Maritime *département*. The full force of winter storm waves thundering against the steep chalk plateau has created towering precipices and bizarre rock formations against a background of alabaster-white cliffs. Most settlements have developed at the river mouths – just a handful of houses or little towns. Interposed between the sea and the foot of the cliffs runs a long strip of coarse, shingle beaches bordered by mussel-clad rocks and tiny tidal pools littered with driftwood and seaweed, while at the cliff top a cool wind blows across the open meadows where seagulls perform their graceful aerobatics.

This route runs parallel to the English Channel, but the first 20km (12 miles) follow a northeastern course inland through gently undulating farmland. Etretat can be reached by bus from either Le Havre or Dieppe. Le Tréport (*see page 33*) is the rail terminus of the Atlantic coast line for Paris–Gare du Nord via Aumale and Eu.

29

Sights

Cap d'Antifer has become a paradise for windsurfers ever since the deep-sea harbour was constructed to accommodate supertankers unable to enter Le Havre.

   ★★ **Etretat** (pop. 1,500), hemmed in between steep cliffs, has for a long time enjoyed a reputation as an up-market holiday resort. Out of season, life in Etretat fol-

Etretat

Beauty on the beach

lows a steady pace, but the breathtaking scenery attracts thousands of visitors during summer and the surge of traffic often brings the town centre to a halt at weekends.

Sights in Etretat include the **Promenade** with views in both directions along the coast. Thursday is market day in Etretat and the medieval **market hall** in **Place du Maréchal Foch** is, like the one in Dives-sur-Mer, constructed from coarsely-hewn beams. Souvenir shops and boutiques now monopolise the space.

The market hall

30

The six bays with Romanesque decorations and the crossing lantern may draw some visitors to the church of **Notre-Dame** in Avenue Nungesser et Coli, but it is the stunning natural scenery that attracts most people and there are three walks to choose from.

At low tide a stroll from the western end of the promenade leads down across the steep shingle beach to a huge cave. While the bizarre rock formations look so fascinating, they are only accessible at low-water and seaweed and eelgrass can create a dangerously slippery surface. The adjoining oyster beds were laid before the French Revolution. A 60-m (200-ft) ladder leads up to a gallery with access to the ★★ **Falaise d'Aval** with an incomparable view along the stony beach and beyond.

The second walk follows the same direction but runs high above the steep bank along the clifftop.

For the third walk head east from the harbour up to the ★ **Falaise d'Amont**, on which stands the church of Notre-Dame-de-la-Garde with its splendid panoramic view over the town and coastline. A memorial and a small museum the **Musée Nungesser et Coli** (tel: 02 35 27 07 47; open daily June to September) commemorate the achievements of the pioneering French aviators Charles Nungesser and François Coli who lost their lives attempting to cross the Atlantic in 1927.

Boules at Falaise d'Amont

The coast road to Fécamp passes through **Bénouville**, where walkers can park their cars and make their way through well-cropped meadows to the coast some 1.5km (1 mile) away. Steps lead down to the strangely weathered beach at **Valleuse du Curé**. Take care after wet weather as the steps can be slippery.

Picturesque Yport

Vaucottes and **Yport** are small seaside resorts with shingle beaches. The latter with its colourfully painted boats presents a picturesque sight. Carthaginians may even have settled here, but certainly this region and **Fécamp** (pop. 20,800) were inhabited well before recorded time. Celts founded settlements on the cliffs before the area came under Roman influence. A monastery was established in the 7th century and pilgrims came to a shrine where drops of Christ's blood were kept. According to legend, persecuted Christians concealed the blood in the trunk of a fig tree and then cast it into the sea to be washed ashore at Fécamp.

The monastery was plundered and destroyed by the Vikings but the Duke of Normandy, Richard I ordered it to be rebuilt and consecrated under the name St Trinité. In 1003, Richard II, the then Duke of Normandy, requested the reformer Guillaume de Volpiano to take over the monastery, which soon became a cultural and spiritual focal point within the duchy.

Fécamp monastery

The church of ★★ **St Trinité** with its 64-m (210-ft) crossing tower has undergone many changes since the days of Richard I, but the Romanesque building impresses mainly by its dimensions. Measuring 128m (420ft) in length, it is certainly the biggest in France. The lantern tower rises in a sweep above the crossing. The Precious Blood relic is kept in a marble tabernacle created by the Italian sculptor Viscardo in 1507. The church is the last resting-place for Abbot Volpiano (fourth chapel) and the Normandy dukes Richard I and II (baptismal chapel).

Apart from the church itself, another of the monastic community's legacies is a yellowish liqueur which brother Bernardo Vincelli first distilled in 1510. Full-scale production of the monks' distillation was later taken over by Alexandre Le Grand who built a factory and named it the ★ **Palais Bénédictine**. It is situated at 110 rue Alexandre Le Grand and the architecture displays a clever blend of Gothic, Renaissance, Baroque and Rococo styles. Guides will explain the various stages of the production process. The adjoining museum houses a collection of medieval art, including paintings, wood and ivory carvings and furniture. (Open 8 February to 4 April 10.30–11.45am, 2–5pm; 5 April to 4 July 10am–noon, 2–5pm; 5 July to 31 August 10am–6pm; 1–28 September 10am–noon, 2–5pm; 29 September to 31 December 10.30–11.45am, 2–5pm; last admission 1 hour before closing.)

Notre-Dame-du-Salut

There can be scarcely anywhere else on the coast road where the view along the cliffs is as striking as at the village of **Senneville**. The panorama near the chapel of **Notre-Dame-du-Salut** provides a superb view worthy of any calendar over the precipice and along the cliffs. On a clear day the view along the winding coastline extends as far as Etretat. Narrow valleys, like carved notches on the edge of a table, have cut their way through to the sea to create space for coastal settlements such as **Les Grandes Dalles** and **Les Petites Dalles** where there is just about enough space to turn a car round. More room is available in **Veulettes-sur-Mer**, located at the mouth of the river Durdent. The main source of employment here is no longer the land or the sea, but the nearby Paluel nuclear power station.

Les Grandes Dalles

Original furnishings in Château de Cany

Les Galets

Varengeville-sur-Mer

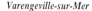

St-Valéry-en-Caux (pop. 5,000) has been a popular centre for sailors for many years and the amateur mariners can be seen at the Friday market stocking up on provisions for the next leg of their voyage. Inland, set in parkland on the banks of the Durdent, lies **Château de Cany** (1 July to 1 September, daily except Friday 10am–noon, 3–6pm). The special charm of this building in magnificent Louis XIII style (1610–43) lies in the combination of bright stone and reddish-brown bricks and also in the fact that it is surrounded by a moat. The interior with its Flemish tapestries and original furnishings is also well worth a closer look.

Veules-les-Roses (pop. 800) is referred to by the local tourist office as a 'mini-Venice' and this may overstate the description a little, but it is situated at exactly the spot where the river Veules flows into the sea. Above the town, a weir stems the flow of the narrow watercourse to create a watercress jungle. Secluded footpaths follow an arm of the Veules along lines of pretty back gardens.

If now is the time for a bite to eat, then **Les Galets** restaurant is worth seeking out (à la plage, tel: 02 35 97 61 33, fax: 02 35 57 06 23). Do not leave without sampling the chef's speciality, a perfect lobster omelette.

Rather like Bénouville, to get to the stony beach in **Sotteville-sur-Mer**, it is necessary to descend 230 steps. Between the weirdly-shaped rocks, enthusiasts can extend their knowledge of sea fauna and flora or collect mussels and starfish.

Varengeville-sur-Mer (pop. 1,000) is only a small village but has more to offer the visitor than many of the other resorts and fishing villages along this section of the coast. Although it may only be viewed from the outside, the ★ **Manoir d'Ango** (April to October daily 10am–7pm, November to March weekends and holidays only) is a splendid example of a Renaissance manor-house. It was built by Italian craftsmen in the 16th century for the ship-builder and shipowner Jean Ango. Much of the building material was specially imported from Italy. In the inner courtyard stands France's largest and most famous dove-cote. The brick and stone facing are arranged in an intricate geometric pattern.

Parc Floral du Bois des Moutiers

In the nearby 10-ha (25-acre) ★ **Parc Floral du Bois des Moutiers** (daily from Easter to All Saints' Day, 10am–noon, 2–6pm), Atlas cedars and oaks, colourful magnolias, camellias, azaleas and rhododendrons thrive in the silicon-rich soil especially lovely in the spring.

The view from the St-Valéry Romanesque church high above the cliffs is worth the climb and in the graveyard, the resting-places of three artists can be found: the painter Georges Braque (1882–1963), the writer Georges de Porto-Riche (1894–1930) and the composer Albert Roussel (1869–1937).

Pourville at the mouth of the river Scie is the last village before Dieppe (*see page 34*), but as a favourite summer retreat for many Parisians, it is sometimes referred to as the '21st Arrondissement'. It may be that they are drawn to the resort in the same way that the impressionist painters Auguste Renoir and Claude Monet were at the turn of the century.

The modest resort of **Puys** lies to the northeast of Dieppe and like Pourville was also a meeting-place for artists. Alexandre Dumas, author of *The Count of Monte Christo* and *The Three Musketeers*, died here in the home of his eponymous son (1824–95), a famous painter. Visitors to their home included the composer Claude Debussy who spent two summers with the Dumases.

Berneval-le-Grand

Berneval-le-Grand can also claim to have an artistic past. The clear light was an inspiration for the paintings of Auguste Renoir and the English writer Oscar Wilde sought refuge here after he had spent two years in prison for homosexuality.

The Alabaster Coast ends at the border with Picardy which is marked by the river Bresle. It flows into the sea at **Le Tréport** (pop. 6,300) which lies to the east of the river mouth. The neighbouring town of Mer-les-Bains is strictly speaking no longer in Normandy, but there is a fine view of Le Tréport's fishing port and the town's narrow lanes from in front of the station. The church of St-Jacques dominates Le Tréport's promenade and busy harbour. It is of late Gothic construction and possesses a fine *pietà* as well as some interesting votive plaques. High above the rooftops at the end of a long flight of steps stands the ★ **Calvaire des Terrasses**, an excellent panorama on the edge of the chalk cliff. Most visitors, however, are attracted to the beach and the little town also boasts some excellent fish restaurants in Quai François 1er.

Le Tréport

Route 5

Dieppe: the starting point for French explorers

Visitors to the busy coastal resort, fishing and passenger port of Dieppe with its 40,000 inhabitants may well be unaware that, centuries ago, intrepid mariners set forth from this town to the then unexplored corners of the world. Men such as Jean Cousin, Thomas Aubert, Pierre Le Moyne d'Iberville and the Parmentier brothers said farewell to their families and explored as far afield as the island of Sumatra, the mouth of the Amazon, the St Laurence River and the Mississippi Delta. Seafaring in Dieppe has changed considerably since those days with modern roll-on roll-off cross-channel ferries now bringing thousands of British holiday-makers and day-trippers right into the town. Since 1994 a new ferry terminal has diverted the heavy traffic from the Avant Port – now a yacht marina.

Café life in the city centre

There is a direct rail link from Dieppe to Paris via Rouen. The CNA company runs bus services east to Le Tréport and west to Fécamp. A bus service from St-Valéry-en-Caux to Rouen connects with a service to Dieppe. There is a year-round ferry service from Newhaven, while Hoverspeed has a seasonal fast craft service.

On the waterfront

History

It is no accident that the word 'Dieppe' resembles the English word 'deep'. Early mariners identified the inshore waters and river mouth nearby to be both deep and safe and the banks soon developed into a thriving port. Dieppe played an important part in sustaining William the Conqueror in power after the Battle of Hastings in 1066 and enjoyed great prosperity up to the 17th century. The town also owes a considerable debt to Jean Ango II (1480–1551). His ships sailed the world and brought riches back to their home port. The Florentine Giovanni di Verrazano served under Ango and later went on to discover the site of what was to become New York.

The Wars of Religion and plague epidemics put a brake on further prosperity and a bombardment by the English navy in 1694 resulted in the almost total destruction of the town and its wooden houses. The fishing industry and the growth of lace-making in the 18th century helped to reverse the town's declining fortunes. The fashion for sea-bathing in 1824 brought wealthy visitors to the town and by 1860 as many as 3,000 English holidaymakers were coming to the resort each year.

In August 1942, a force of 6,000, mainly Canadian, troops failed in their attempt to recapture Dieppe from the Germans. Over 1,000 soldiers lost their lives.

The sights

The ★ **panorama** ❶ on the edge of the cliff above the old castle is easy to reach if approaching Dieppe from the south or west. From this position above the town, it is clear that Dieppe – nestling between steep cliffs at a point where several small rivers, including the Eaulne, Béthune, Varenne, Arques and Scié join the sea – is indeed the perfect place for a port.

As early as the 17th century, Dieppe fishermen became suppliers of fresh seafood to the French court. Scallops from Dieppe are still regarded as a delicacy among discriminating gourmets.

The ★ **Vieux Château** ❷ or old castle dominates the western end of the town (open daily June to September 10am– noon, 2–6pm; October to May till 5pm, closed Tuesday). The huge 15th-century structure with defensive towers at each corner was built by the master fortress builder Vauban and has been altered on many occasions. Initially it was the home of the town's governor, but was later converted into barracks. In 1923 the municipal museum (**Musée du Château**) took over the site and with the fine collection of ivory carvings it earned a reputation

The Vieux Château is famous for its ivory

35

DIEPPE

0   300 m

Newhaven

Notre-Dame de Bon-Secours

Boulevard du Maréchel - Foch

Rue de la Rade

Boulevard de Verdun

Rue Desceliers

Quai Henri IV

Avant-Port

Grande Rue du Pollet

Quai du Carénage

❽ LE POLLET

R. du Haut Pas

R. de l'Epée

Place ❺ Nationale

❶ ❼

Pont Jehan Ango

Casino

❿

❾

Grand - Rue

Rue St-Remis

Rue St-Jaques

❻

St-Jacques

QUARTIER ST-JACQUES

❶

❷

Vieux Château et Musée du Château

Rue de Sigogne

❹ St-Rémy

❸ Place du Puits-Salé

Rue de la Barre

Rue d'Ecosse

Duquesne

Port de Pêche

Arrière-Port

Rue C.-Groulard

Boulevard Gen.-de-Gaulle

Rue du Fg-de-la-Barre

Av. Gambetta

Rue Jehan-Veron

Blvd Joffre

Rue J.-de-Blainville

R. Thiers

Blvd G.-Clemenceau

Gare

La Pénétrante

Bassin du Canada

Rouen, Le Havre

Place du Puits-Salé

Charcuterie

Salut! – Port de Pêche locals

Washing in Le Pollet

far beyond the town itself. As early as the 14th century, Dieppe mariners had been returning from the West African coast with the 'white gold'. Skilled artisans carved both religious and everyday objects out of this precious material and Dieppe became the European centre of the ivory trade until well into the 19th century.

In the centre of **Place du Puits-Salé ❸** in front of the Café des Tribunaux stands a well and, as the name suggests, it was a source of salt water. A few yards away stands **St-Rémy** church **❹**. The Wars of Religion delayed its completion, but it was between 1552 and 1645 that most of the work was undertaken. It has suffered damage on a number of occasions and has always been restored, but little of the original remains, apart from the Gothic choir and the Louis XIII-style facade.

The busy, traffic-free **Grande Rue** – a continuation of Quai Henri IV – links the Place du Puits-Salé with the port. Traditional *charcuteries* and long-established butchers' and bakers' shops stand alongside T-shirt shops and fashionable boutiques to create a lively thoroughfare. A monument in the **Place Nationale ❺** commemorates Abraham Duquesne (1610–88), who commanded the French fleet under Louis XIV.

The church of ★ **St-Jacques ❻** (open daily) has the appearance of a guide book on ecclesiastical architecture. The oldest, Gothic sections are the remains of an earlier building which was largely destroyed by Phillip II's soldiers around 1195. While much of the exterior is Gothic in style, parts of the interior, mainly the choir, Lady Chapel and sacristy, are in the Flamboyant or Renaissance style.

Pont Jean Ango ❼ separates the **Avant Port** (yacht marina) from the **Port de Pêche** (fishing port) and links the commercial heart of Dieppe with **Le Pollet ❽**, the fishermen's quarter with narrow alleys and small cottages.

High above this eastern suburb stands the ★ **Chapelle Notre-Dame-de-Bonsecours**, with a fine view over the rooftops to the chalk cliffs in the west. Votive tablets inside provide an insight into the fears and anxieties of fishing families. Northeast in the old fishing quarter is the extremely popular **Cité de la Mer** (37 rue de l'Asile Thomas, tel: 02 35 06 93 20; open daily May to August 10am–7pm; September to April 10am–noon, 2–6pm). Opened in 1992, the life of the sea is showcased in fascinating, state-of-the-art displays and aquariums.

Most of Dieppe's cheaper restaurants are to be found on the Quai Henri IV along the northern side of the ferry harbour, while the open spaces on the seafront are bordered by **Boulevard du Maréchal Foch** close to the beach and the **Boulevard de Verdun** which runs in front of the hotels, the remains of the town's fortifications, the **Porte des Tourelles ❾** and the **casino ❿**.

Route 6

The rustic charm of Pays de Bray

37

The Pays de Bray:
Le Tréport – Gisors (120km/74 miles)

If cider and apple brandy are synonymous with the Calvados region (*see page 49*), then the Pays de Bray means cheese. Best known among them is the cheese from Neuchâtel. Fresh spring water flows into rivers and streams, lush broad-leaf forests flourish in the valleys and hollows and spa towns such as Forges-les-Eaux prosper from the mineral-rich water in which Louis XII, Queen Anna of Austria and Cardinal Richelieu relaxed.

Away from the little towns and villages, the green meadows and pasture land of the Bray country have changed little from the days when kings, queens and distinguished French statesmen came here to take the waters. It is safe to assume that savouring the famous local cheeses was just as important to these pillars of church and state as the health cures and casino.

For many years the Pays de Bray, snuggling between the plains of Picardy, the Pays de Caux and Normandie-Vexin, was known as Paris's 'pretty farmyard' and any Frenchman who orders a *café au lait* on Boulevard St-Michel in the heart of the capital will know for certain that the milk flowed from the udder of a Normandy cow with black patches around each eye – as if the farmer had fitted a pair of sunglasses.

Forges-les-Eaux (*see page 39*) is at an important rail junction where the line from Paris to Dieppe crosses the line from Rouen to Amiens. CNA buses run between Rouen, Forges-les-Eaux and Aumale. If making for Gisors (*see page 40*), the D921 which runs due south of the town is a more interesting route than the D915.

*William and Matilda
on their wedding day*

Notre-Dame-et-St-Laurent

Château de Mesnières-en-Bray

Sights

Only 3km (2 miles) inland from Le Tréport in the Bresle valley lies the town of ★ **Eu** (pop. 8,000). It was here that Rollo, the first duke of Normandy, died in 932. And when William the Conqueror married his cousin Matilda of Flanders in 1050, the couple chose Eu as the setting for the great event. The inscription on the roughly-hewn rock in **Place Guillaume-le-Conquérant** is a reminder of the wedding, while the castle in which the festivities were held stood only a few yards away.

That site is now occupied by the Renaissance **Château d'Eu** which was begun in the second half of the 16th century. It was a favourite residence for French king Louis-Philippe, who entertained Queen Victoria and Prince Albert here in 1843 and again in 1845. Some of the rooms are given over to the **Musée Louis-Philippe** (open mid-March to early November Wednesday to Monday 10am–noon, 2–6pm; tel: 02 35 86 44 00), which houses a mixture of old masters and contemporary furniture. The **Chapelle du Collège** was built by Catherine of Cleves in 1620. Her mausoleum is on one side of the altar. On the other is that of her husband, Henri Guise, who was murdered on the orders of Henry III.

Opposite the castle stands the church of ★ **Notre-Dame-et-St-Laurent**. Dating originally from the 12th and 13th centuries, it was fully restored in the 19th century. The triple-naved interior with the main nave divided up with arcades, triforium and loft serves as a perfect example of early Gothic. The ambulatory consists of a number of chapels each decorated with sculptures. The superstructure of each chapel is for structural reasons secured by a network of arched buttresses. Behind the altar lies the tomb of the archbishop of Dublin, Lawrence O'Toole who died in Eu in 1181. The crypt is guarded by stone carvings of the dukes of Artois.

Glass-making has a long tradition in the Bresle Valley and in **Blangy-sur-Bresle**, the **Verrerie Waltersperger** in Avenue de la Gare offer guided tours of the factory. Visits are arranged through the Syndicat d'Initiative in Blangy (tel: 02 35 93 50 68). Glass-blowers can be watched at work by the furnace. Some products are produced using traditional methods, but a wide range of the company's glassware is produced using automated equipment. The Waltersperger factory specialises in small perfume and spirit bottles made from coloured crystal glass. Other glass factories in the area concentrate on making test tubes for the pharmaceutical industry.

Northwest of Neufchâtel-en-Bray in the Béthune valley lies the ★ **Château de Mesnières-en-Bray** (tel: 02 35 93 10 04; 1 April to 1 November Saturday and Sunday 2–6.30pm), which resembles some of the châteaux in the Loire Valley, especially Chaumont (sur Loire). With a pointed round tower on either side of the entrance steps, this castle, which was built by Louis XV, appears to be a combination of a fortification and country house. The interior of this magnificent building, which is now used as a boarding school, is the outstanding architectural masterpiece of the Bray region. Its salient features include the **Salle des Cartes** with its 17th-century works of art, which are painted not on canvas but on wood, and the 16th- and 19th-century chapels. The older of the two is decorated with some delightfully carved wooden statues representing Christ, John the Baptist and the four apostles.

Neufchâtel-en-Bray (pop. 5,400) was badly damaged in 1940 and only a few original buildings remain. The oldest parts of the church of **Notre-Dame** date from the 12th century and the 400-year-old nave and splendid stained glass windows make a visit worthwhile. A manor house contains the **Musée d'Art Régional**, where tools of cheese-, clog- and saddle-makers can be seen.

Neufchâtel is known throughout France for a delicious cheese which is marketed under the same name and sold in a variety of shapes. There is a Fête de Fromage held annually on the third weekend in September. Sadly many small-scale farmers using 'traditional' methods have seen cheese production fall into the hands of large dairies, such as those in Neufchâtel, which use state-of-the-art technology in the cheese-making process.

A few farms continue to use traditional methods to make the local cheese (for more information on Neufchâtel cheese, contact the Syndicat Professionel du Fromage de Neufchâtel, tel: 02 32 97 53 01). Two of them are just a short distance from Neufchâtel and are happy to open their doors to visitors. A telephone call in advance is appreciated. M. Brianchon, Ferme des Fontaines, Nesle-Hodeng (on the D135), tel: 02 35 93 08 68 (March to November); M Auvre, Mesnil-Mauger (on the D120), tel: 02 35 90 41 22.

Forges-les-Eaux (pop. 3,800) was once a famous spa town and attracted many celebrated guests. Today the little town is a quiet but refined oasis in an area otherwise dedicated to farming. Iron deposits were discovered by the Romans who used them to make weapons, but at the beginning of the 16th century the town began to prosper when the healing qualities of the mineral springs were acknowledged and bathing in the waters became a fashionable pastime for the wealthy. Louis XII, Anne of Austria and Cardinal Richelieu were convinced of the water's powers. Forge-les-Eaux's reputation as a spa town thus became well established and, centuries later, visitors still come to 'take the waters'. The **Grand Casino** is another major attraction and not just for spa guests. Voltaire is said to have tried his luck at the original casino.

Back to the soil in Neufchâtel-en-Bray

39

A sign of fine cheese

The Grand Casino

BRITAIN

FRANCE

Paris

Route 7

In the footsteps of Richard the Lionheart through Normandie-Vexin:
Gisors – Giverney – Rouen (120km/75 miles)

The region known as Normandie-Vexin lies to the south-east and only just inside Normandy proper and yet in the 10th century it was at the heart of the duchy. Later on, Richard the Lionheart sought to protect the eastern and southeastern flanks against French intrusion and the solid fortifications he created bear witness to this time.

Two's company

Vernon is on the Paris to Rouen railway line. Bus services connect Vernon, Evreux, Gaillon, Les Andelys and Gisors.

Gisors' bold Château Fort

Sights
★ **Gisors** (pop. 9,000) is only a small town, yet as the capital of the Normandie-Vexin region, it can look back to a stirring past. The most important factor in the town's development was its strategic position, on a hill above the Epte Valley on the southeastern edge of Normandy and 900 years ago this was considered an ideal location for a fortress with which to secure the French/Norman border. The castle or ★★ **Château Fort** (open Wednesday to Monday from Easter until the end of September) which overlooks the town and dates from 1097 owes its existence to the then king of England and duke of Normandy, William II, William the Conqueror's son.

Despite the alterations of later years, the castle at Gisors is a fine example of medieval castle construction. The second donjon of the castle – or 'Tour du Prisonnier' was added in the 15th century and famous inscriptions by the inmates can still be seen. The keep and public gardens are located inside a huge ring wall, which was built so solidly that visitors can still safely climb the steps to the 20-m (65-ft) viewing platform.

Among the houses below, the two towers of the church of **St-Gervais-et-St-Protais** are clearly visible. The ceiling and interior were badly damaged during World War II and it has taken many years to restore them to their original condition. Similarly, when the church was started in the 12th century, it took 400 years to complete – hence the juxtaposition of Gothic and Renaissance elements. Despite the range of architectural styles, the church creates a unified, harmonious impression.

Only 15km (9 miles) southwest of Gisors lies **St-Clair-sur-Epte**, the cradle of Normandy. It was here in AD911 that the French king Charles le Simple and the Viking leader Rollo agreed the treaty which laid the foundation for an independent duchy. At that time Rollo controlled the larger part of Norman territory and the treaty officially ceded that land to Rollo. The Vikings, for their part, agreed to stop their violent campaigns and Rollo agreed to adopt Christian beliefs. The church where this treaty was agreed by a solemn oath still exists and on the 1,000th anniversary of the agreement, the village fathers installed a window showing Rollo kneeling at the feet of the king.

For many lovers of art there is no village in France more important than **Giverny**. The impressionist painter Claude Monet lived there between 1883 and 1926 and, soon after his death, the house was turned into the **Musée Claude-Monet** (tel: 02 32 51 28 21; open from the beginning of April to 1 November Tuesday to Sunday 9.30am–6pm). It draws visitors from all over the world. The best time to appreciate the peace and quiet the painter enjoyed is early in the morning before the queues form outside the pink-washed house. The rooms are painted in different pastel shades with light blue, for example, in the reading room and cream in the bedroom where the painter died. The kitchen wall is covered with Delft tiles.

Monet's house at Giverny

The interior has different pastel shades

Most of his attention, however, was devoted to the **garden** where nothing was left to chance. The painter spent hours there with brush and palette in hand creating those world famous paintings which now hang in the top galleries of Normandy, Paris and elsewhere. Opened in 1992, the **Musée d'Art Américain** (99 rue Claude Monet, tel: 02 32 51 94 65; open April to October Tuesday to Sunday 10am–6pm) highlights the works of American artists inspired by Monet.

Giverny is actually only a suburb of **Vernon** (pop. 23,500). For many Parisians this pleasant town is the gateway to Normandy. The French king, Phillip II, must have viewed the town in the same light when he seized it from the Normans in 1204. During the Hundred Years' War Ver-

41

Claude Monet Garden

Stained glass in Notre-Dame

Vieux Moulin

Vernon returned to English rule for about 30 years, before it finally was returned to the French.

In the centre of Vernon stands the church of ★ **Notre-Dame** which was begun in the 11th century but work continued into the 17th century. A superb rose window with elements of Flamboyant style dominates the west front.

The oldest house in the town, known as *Maison du Temps Jadis* (In Days Gone By), will inevitably attract attention. This medieval half-timbered structure is currently used to accommodate the tourist information office. The **Hôtel de Ville** or Town Hall was completed at the end of the last century. A walk through the old town's narrow alleys with their half-timbered houses is to get close to life in the Middle Ages. The **Musée Alphonse-Georges-Poulain** (12 rue du Pont; open 1 April to 31 October Tuesday to Friday 11am–1pm, 2–6pm, Saturday and Sunday 2–6pm only; 1 November to 31 March Tuesday to Sunday 2–5.30pm) displays artefacts of archaeological and regional interest as well as a small collection of paintings, including some by Claude Monet.

Near the Pont Clemenceau in Vernonnet, a district of Vernon, stands one of Normandy's most frequently photographed places, the **Vieux Moulin**. This 16th-century mill has been lovingly restored but it is a private property belonging to an unknown American heir. A few yards further on stands the **Château des Tourelles**. This ruined castle was constructed in the early Middle Ages to protect a bridge which once crossed the river Seine at this point.

The small town of **Gaillon** (pop. 6,300) on the left bank of the Seine is noted for the **Château de Gaillon** (open daily 1 July to 31 August 10am–noon, 2–6pm) which represents a milestone in castle architecture. It suffered badly during the Hundred Years' War and was rebuilt in 1453, but the most significant event in the castle's lifetime is attributed to Cardinal Georges d'Amboise who gave orders for the castle to be converted into a summer residence in Italian Renaissance style. The castle is worth stopping to admire, even if only for the view from the castle forecourt over the tiled roofs to **Les Andelys** in the Seine Valley. Situated high above the river valley, ★★ **Château Gaillard** (open daily mid-March to mid-November 9am–noon, 2–6pm, closed Tuesday and Wednesday mornings) has played an important role in the history of Normandy. It was built in the 12th century by Richard the Lionheart as part of a defensive ring intended to thwart the aggressive intentions of the French crown. Once Phillip II had captured Gisors in 1196, Richard I ordered the construction of this castle as a replacement and it was completed within a year. It remained in Norman hands for only a few years. On 6 March 1204, this proud fortress fell to

Richard the Lionheart's Château Gaillard

Phillip's men, thereby opening up the way through to Rouen. Only parts of the curtain wall and fortress remain.

18th-century market hall, Lyons-la-Forêt

The Normandie-Vexin route leaves the Seine Valley and heads northeast towards the 10,000 ha (25,000 acre) **Forêt de Lyons**. In earlier times, the woods would have echoed to the sound of hunting horns as the dukes of Normandy followed closely on the heels of deer and wild boar. In 1138, in the heart of the forest, Henri I Beauclerc, one of William the Conqueror's sons, founded a Cistercian abbey. However, only ruins remain of the 90-m (295-ft) long and 40-m (130-ft) wide church of the **Abbaye de Mortemer**.

Abbaye de Mortemer

Lyons-la-Forêt (pop. 700) is a small, picturesque centre for walkers, who will find a wide selection of footpaths to choose from. The marketplace is dominated by an 18th-century market hall with a fine timber roof.

The château at **Vascœuil** (open daily 1 April to 16 November 2.30–6.30pm; July and August 11am–7pm) attracts considerable interest from tourists. It was built between the 14th and 16th centuries and was for 30 years the home of the French historian, Jules Michelet (1798–1874).

The château at Vascœuil

The village of **Ry** attracts much greater interest. Students of French literature will recall the fictitious settlement of Yonville in Gustave Flaubert's *Madame Bovary* as it is said that the village was based closely on Ry. A bust of the Norman writer stands in front of the post-office.

The ★ **Château de Martainville** (open Wednesday to Monday 10am–12.30pm, 2–6pm, till 5pm in winter) in **Martainville** has a certain fairy-tale quality about it and, as the last stop on this route, the castle with its pointed towers, dormer windows and brick chimneys is definitely worth a quick look. The building also accommodates the **Musée Départementale des Traditions et Arts Normands** (same opening times as above). On display are late medieval furniture and artefacts from rural life.

Château de Martainville

Route 8

Evreux cathedral and the River Iton

Evreux: The charm of history

Ducks rest beneath tall trees on the river banks, a small bridge crosses the water in a gentle arc and *impatiens* carpet the embankment. Add a picture-frame and a signature to this tableau and it would then be easy to believe that with a few swift brushstrokes Claude Monet had painted the scene.

Evreux is on the Paris St Lazare–Cherbourg railway line. The town is linked by bus to the towns of Vernon, Rouen, Brionne, Conches and Nonancourt.

History

Not everything in Evreux is quite so romantic as the river scene by the River Iton. Centuries of history have left their

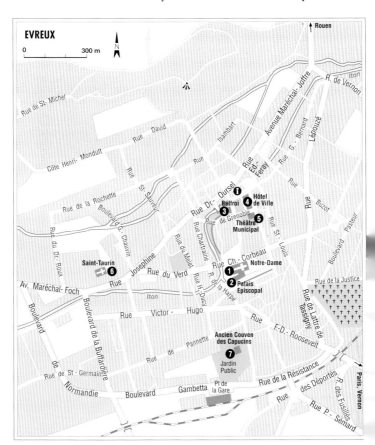

mark on this town of about 50,000 inhabitants. Tales of war and destruction in Evreux go back to the 5th century when Vandals sacked the town, which had been founded by the Romans on the site of a pre-Christian Celtic settlement. In the 9th century the Vikings razed the town and in 1119 the English king Henry I burnt down the wooden town centre. When John, brother of Richard I, seized Normandy, he ordered the massacre of the entire French garrison. In reprisal, Philip II decreed that the town be burnt to the ground. During the Hundred Years' War, the cycle of devastation and reconstruction continued and in World War II, many old buildings were destroyed by bombs.

Sights

The **Cathédrale Notre-Dame** ❶ with its Renaissance-style west façade of niches, ledges and pillars and dissimilar towers is best viewed from the Promenade du Miroir d'Eau. On windless days this image is reflected in the river – a popular theme for photographers.

Cathédrale Notre-Dame, exterior and detail

A passage links the cathedral with the former **bishopric** or **Palais Episcopal** ❷. It stands on the site of fortifications erected by the Romans in the 3rd century and remains can be seen inside the Palais in the **Musée d'Evreux** (the museum has recently been refurbished). Another exhibit on view in the museum is a figure of Jupiter dating from the 1st century BC.

The central business quarter of Evreux has department stores, and many small shops line **Rue du Dr Oursel**. The **Beffroi** (also known as the 'Tour de l'Horloge') ❸ nearby, dating from the 15th century, overlooks the town. This delightful tower rises to a height of 44m (144ft) and in fact consists of two separate towers, each with its own spire. In the higher of the two towers hangs a bell which is almost 600 years old and weighs two tons. In late afternoon the belfry's shadow extends as far as the **Hôtel de Ville** ❹ and the neighbouring **Théâtre Municipal** ❺.

The Beffroi

Saint-Taurin ❻, where the first bishop of Evreux is said to be buried, dates from the 14th century but a closer inspection will reveal sections of the building which date from two to four centuries earlier. One important treasure which the church guards is the splendid St Taurin's Shrine. This masterpiece of French craftsmanship recounts events from the life of the saint. This gleaming reliquary is in the form of a 1.2-m (4-ft) high and 1-m (3-ft) wide miniature chapel and bears testimony to the craftsmanship of French gold and silversmiths during the 13th century.

The perfectly formed cloister in the **Ancien Couvent des Capucins** ❼ dates from the 17th century and serves as evidence of the Capuchin monks' skills. It is not difficult to imagine the brethren picking herbs in the beautiful garden until called to prayer by the bell.

Honfleur harbour

BRITAIN

Paris

FRANCE

Route 9

The Calvados Coast:
Côte de Grâce and Côte Fleurie (32km/20 miles)

The French hosts and their international guests sip apéritifs in the beach cafés, strollers and sun-worshippers parade up and down the wooden platform, while on the restaurant terraces, the secluded world of rural Normandy merges with sophisticated and fashionable metropolitan life to create a world-renowned resort.

The Calvados Coast between the mouths of the Risle in the east and the Orne in the west is a collection of superlatives: magnificent beaches, picturesque harbours and exclusive seaside resorts. For the stretch of coast between Honfleur and Cabourg, the descriptions Côte de Grâce (Coast of Grace) and Côte Fleurie (Floral Coast) can be applied with full justification.

Trains link Paris St-Lazare with Trouville/Deauville via Lisieux, continuing on to Dives-sur-Mer and Cabourg. Connections to Honfleur, Deauville and Caen. Cabourg is served by buses linking Caen and Le Havre via Honfleur. In Honfleur boat trips on the *Vedette Stephanie* depart from Quai des Passagers, tel: 02 31 89 91 49.

Sights

Eating outdoors at the Vieux Port

The harbour or ★★ **Vieux Port** at **Honfleur** (pop. 8,200) forms an inner courtyard surrounded like a castle wall by lines of narrow houses some with seven storeys. At the end of the 15th century, seafarers like Binot Paulmier de Gonneville and Jean Denis sailed off into the unknown on voyages of discovery and on 15 March 1603 Samuel de Champlain set sail from Honfleur in the *Bonne-Renommée* to cross the Atlantic and five years later he founded the Canadian city of Quebec.

If the 16th and 17th centuries belonged to these mariners, then the 19th century was the artists' heyday. Eugène Boudin *(see page 82)* came from Honfleur and his paintings of the sky and the sea paved the way for the impressionists. Boudin rented a room from Mère Tantain in **Ferme Saint-Siméon** (now a very expensive country house hotel) paying 40 francs a month including meals, and with a view from the window over the beautiful coastline, he indulged his passion for painting. Other painters such as Corot, Courbet, Isabey, Troyan and Diaz were also inspired by Normandy's clear light and worked in Honfleur. The **Musée Municipal Eugène-Boudin** in Place Erik-Satie evokes memories of Honfleur's artistic past (open 13 March to 30 September Wednesday to Monday 10am–noon, 2–6pm; 1 October to 12 March Wednesday to Monday 2.30–5pm, Saturday and Sunday 10am–noon, 2.30–5pm; closed January to mid-February).

Ferme Saint Siméon

In the vicinity of the swing bridge, between the inner and outer harbour, stands the **Lieutenance** or Governor's House. Built during the 16th and 17th centuries it was formerly a part of the town's fortifications.

The wonderful wooden **church and belfry of ★ Ste-Cathérine** lies further towards the town centre. Built in 1468, this church contains two identical naves with timber roofs and wooden pillars. Once your eyes have adjusted to the gloom, many fine wooden carvings can be seen. Every Saturday a colourful market occupies the square in front of the church.

Ste-Cathérine

Above the town stands ★ **Le Calvaire** with the chapel of **Notre-Dame-de-Grâce**. This graceful 17th-century building is visited by pilgrims, mainly seafarers, every year. A little higher the Mont-Joli panorama affords excellent views over the rooftops and along the coast.

★ **Trouville-sur-Mer** (pop. 5,600) and Deauville sit on either side of the River Touques and the two towns vie with each for the holiday trade. Trouville is more popular with families than Deauville which attracts well-heeled, international jetsetters. Both resorts have wide, sandy beaches but in Trouville the casino, swimming pool, the **Aquarium Ecologique** (open daily Easter to October 10am–noon, 2–6.30pm; July and August 10am–7pm; November to Easter 2–6.30pm), and water therapy institute also attract many visitors.

Dozing in Deauville

The Pont des Belges connects the two towns across the river. With a population of 5,000, **Deauville** has become one of France's top resorts and certainly the most exclusive holiday centre in Normandy. The main attractions are the Boulevard Cornuché with its white casino

Child's play

Dives-sur-Mer

The medieval market hall

and the wooden plank promenade known as ★ **Les Planches** which runs alongside the swimming pool, tennis courts, mini-golf course and pony club. In the summer, parasols and sunbeds in red and blue set off against the white sand create a *tricolour* effect. Deauville's reputation is due in no small way to the many cultural events such as film and music festivals which draw international names. Major sporting contests include the polo championships, horse-racing and sailing.

★ **Villers-sur-Mer** is situated on the zero line of longitude and a line on the promenade represents the spot. In the world of palaeontology, the town has a special significance as huge numbers of fossils have been found in the chalk cliffs known as the *Vâches Noires* (Black Cows).

The small coastal town of ★ **Houlgate** (pop. 1,700) lies on the east bank of the River Dives and is recognised as an exclusive seaside resort with some superb summer residences along the sea front. In Rue Henri-Dobert, *Columbia, Merrimac, Minnehah*a and *Tacoma*, four American Renaissance-style villas, are the most striking.

Just south of Houlgate the coast road heads inland towards **Dives-sur-Mer**, a small town with a population of about 6,000. It was here in 1066 that William the Conqueror assembled his fleet before setting sail for England. Above the **Notre-Dame-de-Dives** church portal, the names of the 475 men who accompanied the Duke of Normandy on his voyage across the English Channel are listed. The finest building in the central market square is the medieval **market hall** with its well-maintained timber roof. Every Saturday morning farmers, market traders, and customers pack the dimly-lit hall where the tables are laden with fresh vegetables, shiny apples, sausages and crusty bread.

Opposite the market hall stands another historic building, the **Lieutenance**, the former residence of the Lord of Falaise, which possesses a tall, restored façade. It is a shame that aromas of Norman cuisine no longer emanate from the windows of the medieval **Village Guillaume le Conquérant** inn. Instead, a range of undistinguished toys and souvenirs are on sale here.

★ **Cabourg** (pop. 3,400) owes much of its fame to the celebrated writer Marcel Proust (1871–1922). At the beginning of the 1880s, he came to Cabourg in the hope of bringing some relief to his asthma. Only 20 years earlier, the town had been laid out in a geometrical, semi-circular pattern with all the main roads meeting at the square in front of the **Grand Hôtel**. Even in his later years, Proust made his way up to his writing desk in room 414 of the hotel. Cabourg has become a literary monument as a result of Proust's 13-volume masterpiece *À la recherche du temps perdu* in which it features as the town of Balbec.

Route 10

Cider, Calvados and Camembert:
The Pays d'Auge (150km/93 miles)

There is no area of Normandy where it is harder to stay sober than the Pays d'Auge. But it is not alcoholic drinks which are the intoxicants, rather the rolling hills, secluded copses, green meadows, remote half-timbered villages and narrow country lanes which wind through the shady valleys and broad pastures like a roller coaster.

Lisieux (*see page 52*) is on the Paris St Lazare line to Caen and Cherbourg. A branch line links the town with the Côte Fleurie. Bus services link Lisieux with the nearby towns of Pont-l'Evêque, Honfleur, Livarot and Vimoutiers.

Sights

A foretaste of what lies ahead can be found in the village of **Cricqueville-en-Auge**, which lies just to the south of *Cricqueville-en-Auge*
Dives-sur-Mer. Reddish-brown bricks alternate with light-coloured stones to give the castle facade the appearance of an outsized chess board.

49

Better known is the village of ★ **Beuvron-en-Auge** *Beuvron-en-Auge*
(pop. 275). The houses look so immaculate. Perhaps the mayor himself takes a tin of paint and a paintbrush every evening to touch up the beams. Beuvron is one of the *villages préservés* where the villagers care about the upkeep of their old homes. In this case the loving attention extends to maintaining window-boxes of glorious, colourful geraniums – creating an image much appreciated by the visitors and their cameras. Every farmhouse by the roadside sells home-made cheese, fresh butter, calvados and preserves made *à l'ancienne*.

If the displays of home-made produce have whetted the appetite, then the place to go is a Ferme Auberge such as the Ferme-Auberge du Laizon in **Cleville** (signposted from Beuvron), tel: 02 31 23 64 67. Reservation is essential. Even the apéritif of icing sugar, calvados, crème fraîche and a pinch of nutmeg is a revelation, if certainly not low in calories. Choose a main course from rabbit *à la normande* or lamb cutlets which the proprietor grills *Crèvecoeur-en-Auge*
in the dining room as chickens wander in and out through the open door in search of crumbs.

Crèvecoeur-en-Auge (pop. 550) owes its place on the Pays d'Auge sightseeing route to the ★ **Château de Crèvecoeur** (open April to June and September Wednesday to Monday 11am–6pm; July and August daily 11am–7pm; October Sunday 2–6pm). The entrance hall is unusual with coloured stones in a chequerboard pattern

Manoir de Coupesarte

Oil prospecting in the Musée de la Recherche Pétrolière

Livarot Cheese is cone-shaped

typical of the region at the base of the round portal. It is the sort of place where a watchman might at any moment open one of the leaded windows on the upper floor and rudely demand to know who is seeking entry. In addition to the geometrical timber design and cone-shaped, weatherboarded towers at the flanks, there are a number of other buildings which deserve a closer look including the farmstead, barn and dovecote, although the main attraction is the fortress with the Schlumberger museum. The **Musée de la Recherche Pétrolière** is run by the Schlumberger Foundation, whose funds derive from two French industrialists and oil-prospectors.

Grandcamp-le-Château castle is in private hands and its owners shield themselves from prying visitors by a moat and wall, but it is possible to catch a glimpse of the grounds from the small bridge which crosses a pretty stream by the main entrance.

The rustic charm of the ★ **Manoir de Coupesarte** will entrance visitors, who are welcome to view the manor from outside but are really only tolerated in the grounds. It stands in the middle of a man-made lake.

Livarot (pop. 2,500) is not noted for any historical sights, but its cone-shaped cheese has put the little town on the map. The **Musée du Fromage** (68 rue M. Gambier, tel: 02 31 63 43 13) is 18km (11 miles) southwest of Lisieux and shows how cheese used to be made on farms. Locally-produced cheeses and many others are on sale at the busy Thursday market.

A bigger market takes place every Monday in **St-Pierre-sur-Dives**, 16km (10 miles) to the east. The town is a flourishing centre for arable and livestock farmers and the size of the **Halle aux Grains** or Corn Exchange stands as a monument to its founders, the monks from the ★ **Abbaye de St-Pierre-sur-Dives**, who as early as the

13th century recognised the potential of the surrounding farmland. The abbey church was built in the 12th century on the foundations of an earlier Romanesque church. A new section was added in subsequent centuries: the crossing tower in the 13th century, the west front and north tower in the 14th century and the upper part of the nave in the 15th century. This abbey is regarded by many as one of the finest sacred buildings in the whole of Normandy.

A detour to **Vimoutiers** (pop. 5,000), south of Livarot, follows the pretty Vie Valley. In the town's market square stands a monument to Marie Harel, a farmer's wife who is credited with bringing to the attention of a grateful world Normandy's most valuable export, Camembert cheese. The history of the cheese and the story of how it is produced is documented in the **Musée du Camembert** (10 avenue du Général de Gaulle, tel: 02 33 39 30 29; open daily 1 April to 31 October 9am–noon, 2–6pm, Sunday 10am–noon, 2.30–6pm, closed Monday morning; 1 November to 31 March Monday to Saturday 10am–noon, 2–5.30pm, closed Sunday and Monday morning). The building is a reproduction of a cheese-making plant and it has on display many colourful Camembert labels.

Monument to Marie Harel

Musée du Camembert

51

A few minutes to the southwest by car lies **Camembert** itself, a name known as widely throughout the world as the Eiffel Tower, though the village has had to hand over the production of this famous soft cheese to Vimoutiers. The **Ferme de la Héronnière** is a working farm open to visitors, where the traditional methods of cheese production are still followed (daily except Sunday). A phone call in advance is appreciated, tel: 02 33 39 08 08.

The popular Château St - Germain-de-Livet

The moated ★ ★ **Château St-Germain-de-Livet** (open 1 October to 31 March Wednesday to Monday 10am–noon, 2–5pm; 1 April to 30 September 10am–noon, 2–7pm, closed Tuesday, December and January. Guided tours available upon booking, tel: 02 31 31 00 03.)on the banks of the Touques is one of the most popular sights in the Auge Region.

At the entrance to this remarkably beautiful house with chequerboard walls of natural stone and clinker bricks stand two slim cone-topped towers. The roof of the left-hand tower is, for some reason, slightly bigger and it sits on the substructure like an oversized hat. On the right-hand side, the chequered front façade stops abruptly by the entrance to make space for a half-timbered structure with a saddleback roof.

The external promise of St-Germain-de-Livet is almost matched by the interior. To pass from the entrance hall with chimney and Renaissance frescoes up to the upper storey where the original 16th-century tiles cover the floor

The graceful interior

Basilique Ste-Thérèse and monks

and valuable Louis XV furniture is displayed gives some insight into the lifestyle of aristocratic Normans. The Delacroix Room does not house paintings by the eponymous artist, but a collection of his furniture, although he never actually resided in the castle.

Lisieux (pop. 24,500) is the biggest town in the Pays d'Auge and the commercial, industrial and religious centre. Established as a bishopric as early as the 5th century the town and its Carmelite monastery where Ste Thérèse was once a nun have been a place of pilgrimage for decades. All the year round, coach-loads of pilgrims from France and beyond make their *pèlerinage* to Lisieux where the town's shopkeepers who sell plastic saints have been making a comfortable living for many years.

The primary destination for the pilgrims is the huge **Basilique Ste-Thérèse**, dedicated to the nun Thérèse Martin. She was born in Alençon in 1873 and the family moved to Lisieux four years later, living in a house known as Les Buissonnets. As a nine-year-old girl she tried to enter a convent, but was regarded as too young. Five years later, on a pilgrimage to Rome, she was granted a dispensation by the pope and on 9 August 1888 as a 15-year-old novice was admitted to the Carmelite convent in Lisieux. Sadly, her extraordinarily pious life in the convent lasted only nine years. She died in 1897 of tuberculosis, but just prior to her death she wrote the story of her short-lived spiritual pilgrimage, *L'histoire d'une âme* (The Story of a Soul). She was canonised in 1925.

The huge cathedral, built in 1929, was consecrated in her honour in 1954. The architects have, however, not heeded Ste-Thérèse's message of humility and moderation, apparently believing that sheer size is the true measure of all that matters in this life. The basilica, made from white stone, consists of a 95-m (311-ft) high dome, a nave 30-m (98-ft) wide and 37-m (121-ft) high and a number of smaller towers. The result is that the whole building resembles a combination of St Peter's Cathedral in Rome and a Turkish mosque. The crypt is also of vast dimensions with space for thousands of worshippers. **Les Buissonnets** (open daily 9am–noon, 2–6pm in summer, May and June till 5.30pm; 10am–noon, 2–4pm in winter, closed January) in Boulevard Herbert-Fournet is also much visited by pilgrims. It consists of the dining room and bedroom where the young Thérèse lived with her father, brothers and sisters before entering the convent.

Half-timber in Rue Henry-Chéron

Old Lisieux was badly damaged by fire during the battles of 1944 and so the former *capitale du pan de bois* (half-timbered capital) is only visible in a few places, such as Rue Henry-Chéron, Rue du Docteur-Degrenne and Rue Docteur-Lesigne, where the old houses have been rebuilt.

Evidence that Lisieux was formerly an attractive town

with many historic buildings can be found in **Musée du Vieux-Lisieux** (38 boulevard Pasteur) where watercolours, engravings and old photographs are on display.

The church of **St-Pierre** in the town centre stands on a site of historical significance. It was in the original church in 1152 that the Plantagenet king of England, Henry II married Eleonore of Aquitaine, whose marriage to the French king Louis VII had been annulled. This marriage had momentous significance as thereafter large areas of French soil passed to the English crown. Two hundred years later, the consequences of this marriage sparked off the Hundred Years' War in which the English king, Edward III, laid claim to the French throne.

St-Pierre

The modern Eglise St-Pierre was started in the 12th century, but subsequently underwent many changes. As the first Gothic church in France, it has a special place in French architectural history. Bishop Pierre Cauchon who condemned Joan of Arc to death is buried in the Lady Chapel. The old **episcopal palace** which stands next to the church was built in the 17th and 18th centuries and now functions as the *Palais de Justice*. The painted ceiling and the walls lined with gilded Cordoba leather in the **Chambre Dorée** (Golden Room) are well worth a quick look.

The episcopal palace

Pont-l'Evêque (pop. 4,000) is, after Camembert and Livarot, the third small town in the Pays d'Auge noted for its cheese. It lies just a few miles from the Côte Fleurie. This square, soft, creamy cheese has been produced in Pont-l'Evêque since at least the 17th century. Another local speciality is the tasty, pink-fleshed trout which do not need to have their scales removed. The River Touques is one of the best places in France to fish this species.

The 'Père Magloire' distillery in the Route de Trouville produces calvados using the traditional methods. It takes several years for the otherwise colourless liquid to mature and develop the much valued amber tinge. 'Père Magloire' store about 2,000 oak casks in their cellars. As the **Musée du Calvados et des Métiers Anciens** (April to October daily 10am–12.30pm, 2.30–6.30pm) adjoins the distillery, it is possible to sample a drop or two.

Musée du Calvados

On the way from Pont-l'Evêque to the Côte Fleurie, on the side of the hill near the village of **Bonneville**, stands the **Château de Guillaume le Conquérant**, or at least what the ravages of time have left behind. It was from this castle in 1066 that William looked out over the English Channel and decided to launch his attack on England.

The last stop of this tour is at **Touques** with its rows of old houses beneath bowed rooftops. This once important town now stands in the shadow of Deauville. It is said that the murdered Thomas Becket visited the church of **St-Thomas** shortly before he met his violent death.

54

NORMANDY (WEST)
ROUTES 11–15

0   20 km

N

Baie de la Seine

Beach Port-en-Bessin

Courseulles-s.-M.   Langrune-s.-Mer

Arromanches-les-Bains

Riva-Bella

Bayeux   Creully

Fontaine-Henry

Ouistreham

Bénouville

Andrieu

Caen 11

Paris →

12

Caumont-l'Eventé

Villers B.

Orne

Aunay-s.-D.   15

Thury-Harcourt

St-Rémy

Château de Pontécoulant

Clécy

Allière

Pont d'Ouilly

Condé-s.-Noireau

Tinchebray

Varenne

Flers

Briouze

Domfront

Le Ferté-Macé

Abbaye aux Hommes
Preceding page: detail from the Bayeux Tapestry

Stained glass window in the Abbaye aux Hommes

Route 11

Caen: a roman jewel with a smooth, modern finish

Caen has survived military campaigns, wars, rivalry and revolutions and many scars still remain, but to step from the brightness of a summer evening into the peaceful shadows of the Abbaye aux Hommes with its vaulting, arcades, pillars, buttresses, roofs and pointed towers, it is easy to forget the conflicts of recent years and imagine a tranquil scene 900 years ago when the abbey church had just been consecrated.

Caen was once the town where William the Conqueror lived, but its importance now is as a city of the arts, a showpiece of Romanesque style, one of the best towns for shopping in Normandy and, with a population of almost 200,000, the administrative centre of Basse Normandie. A good market is held in the Place St-Sauveur every Friday.

Direct rail connection from Paris to Cherbourg. The 'Bus Verts' link Caen with the Ouistreham terminal, where ferries arrive from Portsmouth, and then continue on to Courseulles via Luc-sur-Mer. A good local bus service operates within Caen and the city is also linked to the bus network which serves Calvados and beyond.

Friendly locals

History

During Gallo-Roman times this settlement in a marshy region on the banks of the Orne was known as Cadomus. It only came to prominence in the 11th century when William the Conqueror chose it as his official residence and built a castle there. When Pope Nicholas II raised the order of excommunication against William, who had married his cousin Matilda of Flanders without papal dispensation, the couple founded two monasteries, the Abbaye aux Hommes and the Abbaye aux Dames – now regarded as the two finest examples of Romanesque architecture in Normandy.

In the next two centuries Caen attracted people from a variety of backgrounds and in 1204 the French occupied the town. However, it was captured by the English in both 1346 and 1417, before it was restored to the French in 1450. In 1432 a university was founded in the town.

A plague took its toll on the population in the 16th century and then the Wars of Religion brought a period of violence to the town, as Protestants and Catholics plundered each other's churches. The town also had to endure difficult times during the French Revolution when it became a refuge for anti-Revolutionary Girondistes as they sought to escape – vainly as it turned out – from the Montagnards' reign of terror.

Like many other Norman towns, Caen suffered badly during World War II, mainly during the two-month battle for the town after the Normandy landings in June 1944. In the years after the war almost the whole of the city centre had to be rebuilt.

57

Sights

On a hill in the centre of the city stands the **château** ❶ (rue Montoir-Poissonnerie). It was built by William the Conqueror in 1060 and in subsequent centuries, it underwent many changes. During the Revolution much of the fortress building was removed, but that was not the end of the citadel's place in history as it played an important strategic role during the battle for the city in World War II and by the end of the siege only a ruin remained.

The château by night

It was rebuilt after 1945 and new cultural centres occupied this prime site in the heart of the city. Two museums were opened and Caen became a focus for the arts. In the **Musée des Beaux Arts** ❷ (daily except Tuesday, 9.30am–6pm), the works of Veronese, Tintoretto, Rubens, Le Brun and Boucher and many other famous 17th-century French and Italian masters are on display. Special exhibitions bring together works by painters such as Monet and Courbet who were inspired by the Normandy landscape. The museum also possesses more than 50,000 engravings as well as an unusual collection of Rouen faiences.

Musée des Beaux Arts

History rather than art is the theme of the **Musée de Normandie** ❸ (open April to September Wednesday to Friday 10am–12.30pm, 1.30–6pm, Saturday to Monday 9.30am–12.30pm, 2–6pm; October to March Wednesday to Monday 9.30am–12.30pm, 2–6pm), which occupies the former governor's residence inside the citadel. Exhibits from the region's prehistory, early years, Gallo-

Musée de Normandie

Roman times and the Viking period are displayed here. Other artefacts which document the region's history include a variety of costumes, tools and furniture.

The oldest parts of the **Chapelle St-Georges** ❹ date from the 12th century, but the chapel itself was rebuilt in the 15th century.

Caen's city centre and business quarter lies beneath the **Porte sur la Ville** on the south side of the castle with the church of ★ **St-Pierre** ❺ directly in the foreground. There can be no doubt that this building is the late Gothic jewel of Normandy. A golden weathercock has topped the 78-m (255-ft) spire for many years, but like so many similar pieces of exposed metalwork its movement has rusted and it no longer turns.

Inside the church the apse beneath the stained glass windows is by far the most interesting feature. The delicate masonry resembles filigree lacework.

How the town houses of Caen would have looked before the war can be seen in the historic **Hôtel d'Escoville** ❻ in Rue St-Jean. The building, strongly influenced by the Renaissance style, was built by a wealthy businessman according to plans drawn up by an Italian

Musée de la Poste

architect. The tourist office is accommodated here. At 52 Rue St-Pierre, behind an ancient half-timbered facade with carved beams, the **Musée de la Poste et des Techniques de Communication** can be found. As well as exhibits from the days of stagecoaches and postilions, early communication systems such as the telegraph are displayed.

Louis XIV

Another fine half-timbered building is the ★ **Hôtel des Quatrans** ❽ in Rue de Geôle (no. 31). This three-storey house with leaded glass panes was begun in the 14th century. The inner courtyard creates an authentic medieval atmosphere.

In the middle of the small but charming **Place St-Sauveur** stands a monument to the Sun King, Louis XIV. The church of **St-Sauveur** with its combination of Gothic and Renaissance deserves a quick visit.

The abbey church of St-Etienne

From the **Palais de Justice** ❾, there is a clear view of one of Caen's two main sights, the ★★ **Abbaye aux Hommes** ❿ with the abbey **church of St-Etienne** (Esplanade Jean-Marie Louvel; guided tours, daily 9.30am, 11am, 2.30pm and 4pm). It represents William's atonement and a gesture of reconciliation between himself and the pope, who had excommunicated the duke from the church after his marriage to Matilda of Flanders. In 1077 the abbey, unsurpassed for its austerity and severity, was consecrated. Ten years later William found his last resting-place here after a riding accident. His tomb is marked, but the grave was ransacked and his bones scattered. Lanfranc, the first abbot and later the archbishop of Canterbury, is generally credited with the design of the Romanesque west front. The Gothic apse with its four belfries was added in the 13th century, together with the two spires to the square towers. These were destroyed by Protestant troops in 1562 during the Wars of Religion, but were faithfully restored in the next century. In the 17th century, a new middle belfry was built to replace a 120-m (393-ft) tower which had collapsed. The monastery building is now used by the city administration as offices and was the work of Guillaume de la Tremblaye, architect to the Benedictine monks of St-Maur.

St Jean: sculpture detail

To reach the Abbaye aux Dames, cross the city centre and shopping quarter, paying a brief visit to the church of **St-Jean** ⓫ on Place de la Résistance. It is a splendid example of late Gothic Flamboyant architecture. A landslide caused the tower to lean slightly.

Abbaye aux Dames

The ★★ **Abbaye aux Dames** or Abbaye de la Trinité ⓬ (guided tours, daily 2.30pm and 4pm) is the sister building to the Abbaye aux Hommes and lies in the east of the town at **Place de la Reine Mathilde**. It owes its existence to Queen Matilda and was built for the same reason as the men's abbey. In 1080, only three years after it was consecrated, its founder was buried in the centre of

Modern windows in La Trinité

the Romanesque church. While the dimensions of the Abbaye aux Hommes seem so impressive when viewed from the outside, the women's abbey is of more modest proportions. The differences in the interior are equally striking. While St-Etienne remains largely true to its original design, the recent restoration of La Trinité has brightened the nave. Some modern features such as a new altar have changed the interior's character and there are divided opinions as to the final effect. Similar doubts arose after a 19th-century restoration was deemed to have upset the architectural harmony of the building.

The convent buildings, which were designed in 1704 by Guillaume de la Tremblaye, survived until the French Revolution. Thereafter it was used as a warehouse but in the last century was converted into a hospital. It is now the seat of the regional council for Basse Normandie.

Created for the 50th anniversary of D-Day in 1994, **Le Mémorial – Un Musée pour la Paix** (Memorial – A Museum for Peace; Esplanade Eisenhower, tel: 02 31 06 06 45; open daily 9am–7pm; 12 July to 24 August till 8pm; Last entry 1hour 15 minutes before closing; closed 6–19 January and Christmas) is a fascinating museum covering events in the 20th century from the World War II including footage of the Battle of Normandy up to today. The final gallery is devoted to winners of the Nobel Peace Prize.

Visitors should note that on summer weekends the tourist office organises a three-hour guided tour of Caen. On Tuesday and Friday in July and August, evening tours lasting an hour and a half visit the best known sights. Reservations can be made in the tourist office.

Le Mémorial – Un Musée pour la Paix

Route 12

Sandy beaches:
The Côte de Nacre and Le Bessin (160km/99 miles)

Time heals many wounds. In the very places where on 5 June 1944 under the cover of night the Allied forces landed to begin the invasion of France, local people join together with guests of every nationality to enjoying the sea and sandy beaches beneath steep cliff faces. There are still many places, however, where history intrudes. The remains of this huge military undertaking – war cemeteries, rusted tanks, memorials and the sections of the man-made harbour of Arromanches – can still be seen. Where once amphibious landing craft fought their way on to the beaches, now brightly painted fishing boats and expensive yachts bob up and down.

Arromanches Harbour

Memories of the war impinge on everyday life in so many ways. The inhabitants of Colleville, for example, have tagged 'Montgomery' on to the name of their village, so that the name of the commander of British ground forces on D-Day would never be forgotten. Less honourable, perhaps, are those who, 60 years or so later, seek to profit from the war by buying and selling medals and uniforms. Violence and war have certainly left their mark on this coastal region, but intellect and culture are in evidence just as much here as anywhere else in France. In the picturesque provincial town of Bayeux, which suffered little damage in 1944, the famous *Bayeux Tapestry* still draws countless tourists every year. They stand and stare in their tens of thousands stunned by this colourfully embroidered story book which depicts William the Conqueror's victory at the Battle of Hastings in 1066.

61

Happy to be back on dry land

Bayeux *(see page 63)* is on the railway line which links Paris, Caen and Cherbourg. A branch line connects Bayeux with St-Lô, Coutances, Pontorson and Mont St-Michel. A good bus service links Bayeux with the Côte de Nacre resorts and Caen.

Sights

The **Côte de Nacre** or the Pearl Coast is how this part of Normandy is often described. The name refers to the section between Ouistreham/Riva-Bella and Grandcamp-Maisy. The hinterland is known as **Le Bessin**, a lush pastureland ideal for dairy herds. In between the two lie villages where one might expect to find tumbledown cowsheds rather than proud Renaissance castles such as Fontaine-Henry. This route starts and finishes in Caen and many will be able to complete it in a day, but a leisurely pace will prove more rewarding.

Port en Bessin

Caen, the administrative centre for Basse Normandie (*see page 56*), lies about 15km (9 miles) from the coast but is linked to the sea by the Canal de Caen à la Mer. The main road follows its course towards the English Channel via **Bénouville**. Here the river Orne and the canal were spanned until 1993 by the historic **Pegasus Bridge**. This point was one of the Allied forces' first objectives and was taken by British parachutists. The bridge is now on view as part of the **Mémorial Pegasus**, which includes an important D-Day museum. Open daily May to September 9.30am–6.30pm; October to mid-November and February to April daily 10am–1pm, 2–5pm.

Pegasus Bridge, symbol of liberation

The origins of **Ouistreham/Riva-Bella** (pop. 6,700) are not entirely clear. The fine beach at Riva-Bella obviously played its part in attracting visitors during the 19th century. A casino and the Institute for Thalassotherapy also helped to boost its popularity. In 1986 a ferry crossing opened between here and Portsmouth. The new museum, **Centre Juno Beach**, opened in June 2003 in preparation for the 60th anniversary of D-Day in 2004 (Voie des françaises Libres B.P., Courseulles-sur-Mer, tel: 02 31 37 32 17; open daily April to September 9am–7pm; October to March 10am–1pm, 2–6pm; closed January; Guided tours at quarter past and quarter to the hour).

Probably the main destination for visitors to this region is **Arromanches-les-Bains** (pop. 500). Its coastal location and fine beaches are not the reason for the interest it arouses, but the part it played in the D-Day landings. 'Operation Mulberry', the construction of a man-made harbour in the bay off Arromanches, was one of the most ambitious schemes of World War II. Pontoons were towed over from the south coast of England and secured to the sea-bed. Once complete with a total of 33 jetties and 16km (10 miles) of floating 'roads', it enabled the Allies to supply the troops with 9,000 tons of material each day. By the end of August over 500,000 tons had been landed, but then other Channel ports became available and the temporary harbour was no longer needed. For a more detailed account of the events of those momentous days, visit the **Musée du Débarquement** Invasion Museum, (open daily June to August 9am–7pm; March to May and September 9.30am–5.30pm; February and October to December 10am–5pm) by the car park near the beach. *Arromanches 360* is a moving film with archive footage of D-Day – showing daily at 10 and 40 minutes past every hour.

Musée du Débarquement

Port-en-Bessin-Huppain (pop. 14,500) is a lively and popular resort. The harbour with brightly coloured yachts and motor boats creates a picturesque scene. Bars and small restaurants overflow on to the pavement and on a fine day there is no better place to relax. For lunch, make your choice from the local *boulangerie* and *charcuterie*

Omaha Beach

and then take the main road to the south of the village where there is a clean and shady picnic site.

The Allied forces code-named the stretch of shoreline off Laurent, Colleville and Vierville-sur-Mer **Omaha Beach** and this turned out to be the scene of one of the landing's bloodiest battles with the American 1st Infantry Division bearing the brunt of the losses. The **American Military Cemetery** in **Colleville** (open daily 9am–6pm in summer; 9am–5pm in winter) was consecrated in 1956. While about 14,000 dead were repatriated to the United States, white marble crosses remember the 9,386 American soldiers who were buried here. Over 300 crosses mark the resting-places of unidentified soldiers. The memorial is laid out as a semi-circular colonnade with a loggia at each end. The 7-m (23-ft) high bronze figure symbolises American youth.

The American Cemetery

There is a tremendous view over Omaha Beach from a panorama which lies between the memorial and the coast. In one or two places, narrow lanes lead down to the beach which is ideal for swimming and sunbathing.

Pointe du Hoc

One of the fiercest battles for control of Omaha Beach took place at **Pointe du Hoc**, an exposed headland and a site of great strategic importance. It is one of the few places which still gives the impression of having been a battlefield – gun emplacements, destroyed bunkers, shell craters and bent metal litter the site. A great deal of blood was spilt here before it was finally captured.

Grandcamp-Maisy lies at the western end of the Côte de Nacre and at low tide on warm days when the sun warms the seaweed and the tiny sea creatures on the mud-flats then the distinctive smell of the sea can pervade the air. The River Vire which flows into the Atlantic here has over the centuries brought alluvial sand down to the shore line creating the ideal conditions for oyster and mussel beds. City dwellers are often puzzled by the sight of tractors on the beach at low tide, but that is the time when the fishermen 'harvest their crop' and the low-lying walls surrounding the beds can be seen in the distance.

For the journey back to Caen from Grandcamp-Maisy, say farewell to the coast and head inland to the region known as Le Bessin. Near **La Cambe** on the RN13 stands a reminder that many German soldiers also lost their lives in the battle for the Normandy coast. Over 21,000 bodies lie buried in the German cemetery.

★★ **Bayeux** (pop. 15,000) is the administrative centre of Le Bessin and offers history with a picturesque backdrop. On the banks of the River Aure, which flows through the heart of the town, two wooden waterwheels recall the days of corn mills and of carpenters who shaped the beams for the half-timbered façades in the narrow lanes, creating a medieval atmosphere. But the sight of tourists is also very much part of the day-to-day scene as the town possesses probably the best known of all Normandy's sights.

In the years which followed the Battle of Hastings, not only was a work of art of great beauty and skill created, but also a unique piece of historical evidence. The *Bayeux Tapestry* documents in precise detail the events leading up to the decisive battle and those that followed. The French call the tapestry ★★ **Tapisserie de la Reine Mathilde** and it is displayed in the **Centre Guillaume-le-Conquérant** in Rue de Nesmond, tel: 02 31 51 25 50 (open daily, 13 March to 30 April, 1 September to 17 October 9am–6.30pm; 18 October to 12 March 9.30am–12.30pm, 2–6pm; 1 May to 31 August and Easter weekend 9am–7pm; closed Christmas and New Year).

Centre Guillaume-le-Conquérant

64

The Bayeux Tapestry

A presentation in an ante-room with sound and pictures help to set the scene and provide the historical context. The tapestry itself is as well protected as the Crown Jewels. Bullet-proof glass keeps curious visitors at a respectable distance and dimmed lights create not only a mystical atmosphere but help to retain the colour of the embroidery.

The tapestry measures about 70m (230ft) long and half a metre (18 inches) wide and the story is told in a series of pictures sewn with coloured wool. It is tempting to draw comparisons with a comic strip, particularly when the faces and figures are studied closely. Helmeted horsemen with shields and swords look down at their spread-eagled opponents. But it is not only the battle, which is depicted in the tapestry. The conflict is presented in a wider context. The illustrations tell, for example, how King Harold on an earlier visit to Normandy renounced his claim to the English throne and how, in scene 17, he saved two Norman

The Bayeux Tapestry

soldiers in St Michael's Bay. Animals, weapons, and erotic scenes fill the borders above and below the main pictures. The degree of detail is quite amazing. Altogether there are 58 scenes with descriptions in Latin and a total of 623 figures, 759 animals and 37 ships and buildings. The tapestry was probably unveiled on 14 July 1077 when the new Bayeux cathedral (*see below*) was consecrated. Who was responsible for the needlework is uncertain, but some evidence suggests that it was commissioned by Odon de Conteville, the then bishop of Bayeux, and finally completed in England. Within its 900-year history, it has only twice left Bayeux. In 1803 Napoleon had it displayed in the Louvre in Paris as part of a propaganda battle with the foe across the English Channel and during World War II the tapestry was hidden away in a variety of places. The loyalty of the inhabitants of Bayeux to 'their' tapestry has been amply repaid. In post-war decades the tapestry has brought to Bayeux not only millions of visitors but a degree of prosperity which would surely have delighted William.

Work started on the ★★ **Cathédrale Notre-Dame** (open daily July to September 8.30am–7pm; October to June 8.30am–6pm) in 1047 and lasted for 30 years until it was completed by Bishop Oddo and consecrated in the presence of William himself. However, further work continued in the ensuing centuries as repairs were needed and account had to be taken of new architectural styles. A new crossing tower was added in the 18th century and topped with a Baroque 'bonnet' but there were serious concerns about the additional weight it imposed on the substructure. In the 19th century the decision was made to pre-empt a possible collapse and the foundations and other load-bearing structures were reinforced and a new spire added.

Bayeux cathedral

The interior of the cathedral is an impressive sight. The main features of interest are the 14th-century side chapels with their magnificently decorated capitals and also the chancel which dates from the 13th century. During restoration in the 15th century a Romanesque crypt was discovered underneath the cathedral.

It is tempting to assume that the tapestry and the cathedral are all that Bayeux has to offer, but that would be to overlook the beauty and atmosphere of the medieval old town with some houses dating from the 14th century. The **Office du Tourisme** is based in one of the oldest houses, a huge three-storey half-timbered structure with a steep roof. Similar houses such as the **Maison du Bienvenue** can be found in Rue de la Jurisdiction. Rue de Quincangrogne, Rue des Ursulines and Rue du Général-de-Dais also contain some fine houses.

For wet days there is a wide choice of museums. A

Office du Tourisme

'combination' ticket from the Centre Guillaume-le-Conquérant includes admission to these museums as well. For those who wish to discover more about D-Day then the **Musée Mémorial de la Bataille de Normandie 1944** (open daily 9.30am–6.30pm in summer; 10am–12.30pm, 2–6pm in winter) in Boulevard Fabian-Ware will be of interest. The **Musée Baron-Gérard** (open daily 10am–noon, 2–6pm) in Place de la Liberté houses exhibits of Bayeux lace and porcelain collections. Bayeux was an important lace making centre between the 17th and 19th centuries and there is still a lace-making school in the town. In the Hôtel du Doyen in Rue Lambert-Leforestier the **Musée Diocésain d'Art Religieux** and **Conservatoire de la Dentelle** (Lace Conservatory; open Monday to Saturday 10am–12.30pm, 2–6pm) contains exhibits of religious art and historical documents. One room recreates the scene in which the 15-year-old St-Thérèse asks the Bishop of Bayeux for permission to enter a convent.

Deep in the Seulles Valley lies the unassuming village of **Creully**, not a place, one would have thought, for medieval castles. The castle here has a massive keep in typical 14th-century military-style architecture with battlements and fortified towers mixed with an ornate Renaissance-style round staircase with a domed roof on the side facing the town, and visitors may well be confused about the building's precise function. The castle has, however, had many owners, including Jean-Baptiste Colbert (1619–83), one of Louis XIV's senior ministers who introduced much-needed but unpopular tax reforms. In mid-1944 the place was taken over by new owners, the BBC. Broadcasters arrived and established a radio station intended to keep British (and German) listeners informed about the progress of the invasion.

Château Fontaine-Henry

Further east along the Seulles Valley lies another medieval building, one often seen on calendars and posters, ★**Château Fontaine-Henry** (open Easter to October Wednesday to Monday 2.30–6.30pm; tel: 02 31 80 00 42). The original building was badly damaged during the Hundred Years' War but was restored by the Harcourt family in the 15th and 16th centuries. The Renaissance influenced the new facade of the castle which, together with the steep saddleback and cone-shaped roofs, as tall as the three storeys beneath, create a striking impression.

Treat yourself at the Château d'Audrieu

Country roads lead back to Caen, the starting point for this route. If thoughts are turning to the next meal, then a small detour to **Audrieu** (south of the RN13 halfway between Bayeux and Caen may resolve the issue of where to eat. **Château d'Audrieu** (tel: 02 31 80 21 52, fax: 02 31 80 24 73) is an 18th-century country house, now a hotel with a celebrated four-star restaurant.

Route 13

Pure Normandy:
A tour round the coast of the Cotentin Peninsula
(354km/220 miles)

It sometimes seems as if the people of this region have had
more than their fair share of misfortune. Their old farm-
houses and homes sometimes resemble mini-fortresses
hastily erected from rough stones. Farmers' bumpy fields
often extend to within a stone's throw of the sea, so that
their crops get a salty tang even before they are harvested.
No point on the Cotentin Peninsula lies further than 50km
(30 miles) from the coast and this proximity to the sea
has made its mark on the people and shaped their character. Some similarities with Brittany are quite striking:
wind-battered coasts, trees bowed by Atlantic storms and
stone-wall field enclosures. Practically everywhere on the
Cotentin Peninsula a fresh wind blows, a free, health-en-
hancing bonus to every holiday.

Three days is the minimum period required for this route
with stops in Cherbourg and Granville recommended.
Both towns are well equipped for summer's tourist influx.
As well as being a major Channel port, Cherbourg (*see
page 69*) is the rail terminus for Paris St-Lazare main
line via Lisieux, Caen, Bayeux and Carentan. Bus services
operated by the STN company connect Cherbourg with
St-Lô via Barfleur, St-Vaast-la-Hougue and Carentan.

Granville (*see page 72*) is the rail terminus for trains
from Paris via Dreux and Argentan. The line from Caen
to Rennes passes through Folligny, 16km (10 miles) east
of Granville. Bus services operated by the STN company
connect Granville with Coutances and with Mont St-
Michel via Avranches.

*Cherbourg is a major
Channel port*

A couple of sea dogs

St-Lô: remains of the town wall

Tempting sign in Carentan

Ste-Marie-du-Mont

Reminders of the Longest Day on Utah Beach

Sights

St-Lô (pop. 26,500) is the administrative centre of the Manche *département*. It lies on a hill above the Vire Valley and makes an excellent start and finish to this tour. Despite its importance within the region, it is not a town usually on the tourist's itinerary. This probably results from the fact that around 90 percent of the town was destroyed during World War II. Only the remains of the old town, known as **l'Enclos**, were left and just the southern wall of the town was rebuilt after the war. The church of **Notre-Dame**, built between the 13th and 17th century, suffered the loss of both its towers, although a late Gothic external pulpit survived.

The 'town of ruins' has, however, retained its reputation for horse-breeding and the **Haras de St-Lô** stud (open mid-July to the beginning of March) owes its existence to Napoleon. Public performances, including demonstrations of working horses take place every Thursday at 10am between the end of July and the beginning of September.

Carentan (pop. 7,500) is often described as the 'Gateway to the Cotentin'. It plays an important part in the regional beef and dairy cattle trade. Every Monday the local farmers bring their stock to the cattle market. The central **Place de la République** with its row of old houses makes an attractive focal point and the pretty 15th-century arcades provide shade and shelter from the sun in the summer months.

The quickest route to the coast is via **Ste-Marie-du-Mont**, but a detour via **Ste-Mère-Eglise**, the first town to be liberated by the Allies, will shed light on an unusual war-time episode. John Steele, an American paratrooper, found himself entangled around the church spire as he landed and was not released for several hours. The **Musée des Troupes Aéroportées** (also known as Musée Airborne, tel: 02 33 41 41 35; open 9am–6pm in summer; 15 November to 15 December 10am–noon, 2–6pm; closed December and January) includes among its exhibits photographs of the occasion, a cargo-carrying glider and other equipment.

The distinctive Cotentin coastal landscape begins with **Utah Beach** near **La Madeleine**. If storm clouds are looming on the distant horizon, then the wide, flat belts of sand with marram grass dunes can resemble paintings by Boudin. In summer this strip of beach becomes a racetrack for sand yachting enthusiasts. It can be fun to watch as the brightly-coloured buggies speed through the shallow water driven by the stiff breeze.

Utah Beach has a gruesome past. Monuments, memorial plaques, howitzers and military vehicles by the roadside are all reminders of the 'Longest Day'. In a bunker half-hidden by sand dune is the **Musée du Débarquement** (d'Utah-Beach; open daily May to September 9.30am–7pm; April and October 10am–12.30pm, 2–6pm; November to March Saturday and Sunday 10am–12.30pm, 2–5.30pm. The wide range of exhibits helps to paint a picture of the battles which accompanied the Allied forces' landing.

St-Vaast-La-Hougue

In contrast the old harbour at **St-Vaast-La-Hougue** (pop. 2,100) can only be described as idyllic. Holiday makers can relax, ignore the long shadows of war, take a sip of Calvados and enjoy the sight of brightly-painted boats bobbing up and down in the sun. St-Vaast is well known throughout France as the source of fine oysters. **Fort de la Hougue** lies in a military zone and is not accessible to the public, but the fortifications on the Ile Tatihou out in the bay may be visited, although there is a limit of 500 visitors per day (June to October, 10am–5pm).

Bustling Barfleur

On a fine day, **Barfleur** (pop. 600) with its huge stone houses by a sheltered harbour could easily be confused with the set of a maritime adventure film, but the fishing nets and piles of lobster pots left to dry on the quayside are proof that this is a busy working fishing port. The small, 17th-century fortified church has clearly withstood the full force of the winter storms. Barfleur's craftsmen have earned the town more than a footnote in the history books. They built many of the ships which took William's army across the English Channel in 1066. In 1194, after his adventures in the Middle East and Europe, Richard I sailed from here home to England.

Just north of Barfleur, country lanes lead down to the coast. At **Pointe de Saire**, a make-shift café offers welcome refreshments and a chance to watch the seagulls' aerobatic displays. Near Gatteville-le-Phare, the **Pointe de Barfleur** Peninsula juts out into the English Channel and the platform of the 71-m (240-ft) lighthouse (Normandy's tallest lighthouse) offers a fine viewing point over the countryside. In the centre of **Tocqueville** stands a bust of the famous statesman and historian Alexis de Tocqueville *(see page 84)*, whose family home lies on the edge of the village behind some tall trees.

The sea is in the locals' blood

On the outskirts of Cherbourg is **Tourlaville** Castle (open all year), the scene of a tragic series of events at the beginning of the 17th century. Thirteen-year-old Marguerite de Ravelet was forced by her parents to marry a man of 45 who cruelly mistreated her. She fled to Paris, seeking refuge with her student brother, but out of vengeance, the abandoned husband accused the two of incest and they were both beheaded on 2 December 1603.

The town of **Cherbourg** (pop. 92,000), at the northern tip of the Cotentin Peninsula, is often quickly bypassed by travellers to and from Portsmouth, Southampton and

Parc Emmanuel-Liais

St-Trinité

The Théâtre on Place de Gaulle

Poole, but if time is available a tour of the town can prove interesting, especially to plant-lovers, gardeners and lovers of the sea. Most visitors are surprised to find the **Parc Emmanuel-Liais** where the displays of azalea and rhododendron are particularly striking in spring. Other sub-tropical species such as camellia thrive in the mild, coastal climate.

Cherbourg is, of course, an important naval base and home to the French submarine fleet. Foreign nationals are not permitted to visit the **Arsenal**, from where France's first nuclear submarine was launched.

Naval vessels and channel ferries no longer monopolise the offshore waters. For several years yachts and motorboats have moored in the marina at **Port Chantereyne**. In **Place Napoléon**, Emperor Napoleon I sits on a bronze horse nearby, pointing tellingly in the direction of England, the country which proved so defiant during the Napoleonic wars.

The basilica of **St-Trinité** in Rue de l'Eglise stands on the site of an earlier church. Its construction and ornamentation is characterised more by Flamboyant than Gothic influences. The altar is baroque, but the tower dates from 1825. However, the main interior attractions are 400-year-old decorations on the upper gallery of the nave. The painted carvings depict scenes from the life of Jesus.

Tuesday and Thursday are market days and the farmers and fishermen meet under the colourful marquees in the **Place de Gaulle**. The tables are invariably weighed down with mounds of fruit and vegetables, smoked hams and mouth-watering tartlets. The neo-baroque facade of the late 19th-century **Théâtre** forms the imposing backdrop for the market scene. Behind the theatre, the **Musée Thomas-Henry** (daily except Monday, 10am–noon, 2–6pm, Sunday 10am–noon, 2–6pm) houses works by Jean-François Millet (1814–75), Hubert Robert (1733–1808) and the Italian artist Angelico (c. 1387–1455).

The **Fort du Roule** on a 100-m (325-ft) hilltop looks down over the rooftops and the view gives a clear picture of Cherbourg's geographical location and an insight into its commercial activities. Against the background of a choppy English Channel, wide avenues, apartment blocks and industrial complexes dominate the foreground. The **Musée de la Guerre et la Libération** (open daily May to September 10am–6pm; October to April Tuesday to Sunday 9.30am–noon, 2–5.30pm) whose exhibits document the Allied landing is to be found in the ramparts.

In 2002, an award-winning attraction opened in Cherbourg. The **Cité de la Mer** (Gare Maritime, tel: 02 33 20 26 26; open daily 1 June to 30 September 9.30am–7pm; 1 October to 31 May 10am–6pm; ticket office closes one hour before the end of visiting hours). Housed in the former Transatlantic ferry terminal, this vast cultural and scientific park is dedicated to man's exploration of the sea. As well as a huge aquarium the other star attractions are *Le Redoutable*, France's first nuclear submarine and the compulsively interactive section on submarine technology.

Cap de la Hague

The road out of Cherbourg to the west heads towards the remotest point in Normandy. Television aerials on rooftops and cars parked beside houses in tiny hamlets surrounded by bleak, hilly countryside are the only signs that the 20th century has reached this part of France. Fresh winds chase the clouds across the broad bay between **Urville-Nacqueville** and **Landemer**. Walkers can follow a rough track towards **Cap de la Hague** and the lighthouse finally marks the weather-beaten tip of the continent.

Anse de Vauville

The less forbidding west coast of the Cotentin peninsula begins at the cape. The deserted **Baie d'Ecalgrain** with its grey sand and black granite curves round beneath the green meadows. The 127-m (416-ft) **Nez de Jobourg**, Europe's highest cliff, juts out like a church pulpit. The winding coast road leads south through **Herqueville** revealing a fine view of the pretty **Anse de Vauville** bay. The little town of **Biville** has two surprises for the unsuspecting traveller. First, there is the 12th-century church where a marble sarcophagus enclosing the glass coffin of the Blessed Thomas Hélye lies. A pilgrimage to the church takes place on 18–19 October. Second, there is the undulating dune landscape beneath the church.

Low tide at Diélette

As the coastline winds its way south towards Mont St-Michel, the distance between high and low water increases. The greatest difference recorded in Normandy is 14m (45ft), exceeded only by the Bay of Fundy in Canada. The little port of **Diélette** is the best place to observe this phenomenon. At low tide fishing boats rest in pools of seawater like beached whales.

The towns of **Carteret** and **Barneville-Carteret** are firmly established tourist resorts. The coastal path here is part of the long-distance GR223 Footpath, known as the *Sentier des Douaniers* (Customs Officers' Path).

Château de Pirou

Lessay lies inland at the mouth of the Ay Estuary. Visitors to the town are inevitably drawn to the early Romanesque monastery church **Ste Trinité** of the former Benedictine abbey (daily, 8am–7pm, guided tours in the summer months at 11am and 3pm). Despite severe damage during World War II, the original stones were used in the restoration work and the church was reconsecrated in 1958. On the second weekend in September, the sleepy town is aroused from its slumbers. Ever since the 13th century, the Holy Cross market has been held here, nowadays attracting traders, performers and hordes of visitors.

To one side of the main road **Château de Pirou** (open daily 9am–noon, 2–6.30pm, closed Tuesday in winter) guards the surrounding area. A legend can perhaps explain the large number of geese to be seen nearby. When the Vikings finally took the castle they were astonished to find just an old man behind the walls. He told the Norsemen that all the other soldiers had turned into geese and flown off and the Vikings said they remembered seeing a flock of geese flying overhead earlier on. Every year the geese return to the Cotentin Peninsula in the hope of finding the book with the instructions for changing them back into men, but the book will never be found as it was burnt by the Vikings during the siege of the castle.

Gothic marvel: Notre-Dame

In earlier times **Coutances** (pop. 13,000) was an important religious and spiritual centre. The old houses cluster around the famous ★★ **Cathédrale Notre-Dame** (open daily 9am–7pm), one of the finest and purest examples of Norman Gothic. The first church was constructed before William acceded to the English throne. It was destroyed by fire in 1218 and rebuilt incorporating the ruins of its predecessor.

En route to Lingreville

For an authentic taste of Normandy visit the *boulangerie authentique* just south of the village of **Lingreville** by the junction of the D20 and D298. This is a traditional bakery adjoining a simple village café and the master baker is renowned for his traditional rustic bread.

The resort of **Granville** (pop. 12,500) is overlooked by a huge rock which is visible from afar. Famed for its casino it is sometimes described as the 'Monaco of the north' and one of its most famous sons was the fashion designer, Christian Dior (1905–57). There is a museum in the clifftop house that was his home, the **Christian Dior Museum** (Villa Les Rhumbs, Jardin Publique, tel: 02 33 61 48 21; open daily May to September). With its rusty anchor chains, lobster pots, nets, gleaming yachts and fishing boats, Granville is predominantly a fishing town.

Grand'Porte

Granville has an unusual past as it was founded by the English in the 15th century. The grand plan was to create a base from which to capture Mont St-Michel, but the scheme foundered and the English were forced to flee after only three years. A walled upper town, now referred to as the **Haute Ville**, grew up on the rock and kept attackers at bay for many centuries. A drawbridge by the **Grand'Porte** allows access to the ramparts from the port. The view from the hill extends inland over the walls and rooftops. The **Iles Chausey** and Mont St-Michel can be seen on the horizon. At the western end of the upper town, a lighthouse on the **Pointe du Roc** marks the northern boundary of St-Michael's Bay.

Route 14

**Wonder of the modern world:
Granville – Mont St-Michel (60km/37 miles)**

Like a ghost ship under sail, a pyramid emerges from the mist. This monastery on a rock is certainly the best known of Normandy's sights; some describe it as one of the wonders of the western world and few are disappointed by what they find. While steeped in its own history, what makes it such an attractive destination is its commanding position on the mud-flats of the Baie du Mont St-Michel.

Avranches (*see page 74*) lies on the Caen–Rennes railway line. A service links Avranches with Mont St-Michel (*see page 75*) and Granville. The nearest station to Mont St-Michel is at Pontorson, but there is a regular bus services linking the two towns.

Sights

The coast road from Granville passes first through the village of **St-Pair-sur-Mer**, after St Paterne (or Saint-Pair) who founded a monastery there in AD540 and set about converting the people to Christianity. The church has an early Romanesque tower and St-Pair's tomb lies in the 14th-century chancel.

Kairon-Plage is a windsurfers' paradise and a little further south lies the pleasant resort of **Julouville**.

The village of **Carolles** with its fine beaches to the north makes a good starting point for short walks. Inland lies the green **Vallée des Peintres** and the GR223, a long-distance footpath, follows the coast as far as **Le Pignon Butor** where a magnificent clifftop view extends north to Granville Rock. From Carolles the cliffs become steeper

73

Mont St-Michel viewed from the Jardin des Plantes

and the view of the distant Mont St-Michel becomes clearer. On a fine day the view from the **Pointe de Champeaux** is superb.

Avranches town walls

Avranches (pop. 10,500) is the largest town in the **Baie du Mont St-Michel** and its history is closely linked with the famous monastery. Bishop Aubert founded a monastery here in the 8th century, but even in the preceding centuries, especially during the Roman occupation, Avranches had been an administrative centre. It was to be taken later by Anglo-Saxons, then by Franks and finally by the Vikings. From the 10th century onwards, strong fortifications were constructed but only the **Tour Baudange** and **Tour de l'Arsenal** remain.

The central square **Place Général de Gaulle** makes a good starting point for a tour of the town, especially as the **tourist office** is situated there and it supplies street plans. On the north side of the square, a signposted flight of steps leads to the **Palais Episcopal** (Bishop's Palace). Built in the 15th century the building has been restored a number of times and the highlight is the foyer with ribbed vaulting. The ★★ **Musée Municipal d'Avranches** (open daily June to September 9.30am–noon, 2–6pm; April and May Wednesday to Monday 9.30am–noon, 2–6pm) occupies some rooms in the nearby Tribunal de l'Officialité. Exhibits include a fine collection of illuminated manuscripts from Mont St-Michel.

74

Musée Municipal, exhibit

From the museum the walk passes the old deanery (26 rue de l'Auditoire) to an open space known as the **Plate-forme**. The cathedral of St-André was constructed here in the 12th century, but collapsed in 1794. Three other churches have occupied the site, the oldest of which was built in the 5th century. A slab at the door of the cathedral reminds visitors that an event of great historical importance took place here on 11 May, 1172. Henry II, King of England, kneeled barefoot in the white robe of a penitent, to offer his public apologies for his part in the murder of Thomas Becket, the Archbishop of Canterbury.

Rue de Lille heads back towards the town centre and is lined by a number of Renaissance houses formerly used by the cathedral clergy.

Follow the medieval cobbles in **Rue Engibault** to the **Maison Bergevin**. This house in a cul-de-sac forms a part of the city wall and is worth a quick look. Around **Rue Pomme d'Or** in the direction of church of St-Gervais lies the old business and artisans' quarter. Pass the 17th-century **Maison aux Gargouilles** (Gargoyle House) in Rue Challemel-Lacour to reach the market square or **Place du Marché**, which is bordered by several historic houses.

In the church of **St-Gervais** with its 74-m (242-ft) grey granite bell-tower, the skull of Bishop Aubert can be seen.

The dent in the bone is said to have been made by the Archangel Michael who had ordered him in a dream to build a chapel on Mont St-Michel. Initially the bishop was unsure of the message, whereupon the Archangel appeared twice more. On the third occasion, to ensure that the instruction was quite clear, he tapped the bishop on the head leaving behind a thumbprint.

From the church, cross Place St-Aubert and head back towards the town hall. Southwest of the town hall and outside the scope of the walk lies the **Jardin des Plantes**. Not only do these botanical gardens contain some unusual plants, but the panorama over Mount St Michael's Bay from the gardens of this old monastery should not be missed.

Jardin des Plantes

★★★ Mont St-Michel (Abbey: open daily 2 May to 31 August 9am–7pm; 1 September to 30 April 9.30am–6pm; last admission one hour before closing; closed 1 January, 1 May and 25 December; the monastery itself may only be viewed as part of a conducted tour taking in the abbey buildings, St Aubert's Chapel, the abbey church, the church of Notre-Dame-sous-Terre, the Merveille and the magnificent cloister).

If a piece of heaven landed on earth, then it was Mont St-Michel. This monastery perched on a rocky island in a desert of sand stands as a timeless monument to human hopes and aspirations. Centuries ago pilgrims flocked here from all corners of Europe to save their souls – at that spot where heaven and earth seemed closer together than anywhere else on earth and neither poverty nor frailty prevented the faithful from making the journey.

And today? This illuminated fortress of faith which glows in the darkness like a beacon has lost none of its awe-inspiring dignity and greatness. As soon as day dawns

75

Today's pilgrims

'God's Pyramid'

Battlements of Mont St-Michel

Archangel Michael

The cloister

No shortage of souvenirs

in the east over Avranches, the first cars and coaches start to move across the causeway. 'God's Pyramid' becomes an ant-hill overrun by tourists. Hundreds of thousands visit every year, but the numbers who visit in search of divine consolation are few. In 1966 the Abbey celebrated its millennium and it was returned, symbolically to the Benedictines, who still have a presence here today.

It was just a rough rocky outcrop 900m (2,950ft) long and 78m (255ft) high, when in AD708 – so the legend goes – Aubert, the bishop of Avranches, was instructed in a dream by the Archangel Michael to build an oratory or small chapel at the summit. Many years after Aubert's death in 966, a Benedictine monastery was founded there at the insistence of the then Duke of Normandy, Richard I. Thirty monks first built a pre-Romanesque church over the oratory. This was later to form the **Notre-Dame-sous-Terre** (Our Lady below Ground) when an enlargement of the church above reduced its status to a crypt. The consecration of the abbey church in the 11th century completed the first phase.

The second phase started in 1180 and lasted for a further 20 years, involving the construction of a monastery in Romanesque style, a residence for the abbot, a refectory, guests' hall and almshouse. The third and grandest phase in Gothic style started at the beginning of the 13th century. The architects set about creating ★★ **La Merveille** (the Marvel), the east and west wings of the monastery, justifiably described as an architectural masterpiece. Two storeys of this building were to consist of a guests' hall and knights' hall, while the refectory and ★★ **cloister** occupied the third floor. By the time this final phase was completed, Mont St-Michel had become one of the most sacred places in the whole of France, but it took on a new role as a military abbey. A garrison was stationed here and increasing attention had to be given to fortifications.

More alterations were made, followed by a less strict regime for the monks. Slowly the monastery declined in importance, a process which was accelerated by the French Revolution. In 1863 it was converted into a prison and it was only in the final years of the 19th century that the pointed steeple was added to the abbey church.

Today, Mont St-Michel draws in excess of 1.5 million visitors a year. In high season the massive car park is always full and the smell of sugared *crêpes* or spicy *merguez* sausages dominates the Grande Rue. The route to the summit leads through the **Porte de l'Avancée** main entrance, up the **Grande Rue** along the ramparts to the **Grand Degré** steps, but if you prefer to wait for the coach parties to disperse, a stroll round the huge rock underneath the ramparts can be very rewarding.

Route 15

Foundrymen and coppersmiths with Swiss accents:
Mont St-Michel – Suisse Normande – Orne Valley –
Caen (150km/93 miles)

Rolling countryside generally characterises Normandy but
there are one or two hilly regions of which the **Suisse Normande** is the most popular. Swiss Normandy lies just south
of Caen. This delightful valley has been carved by the
River Orne and has created an area ideal for such activities as walking, mountaineering, canoeing or cycling. To
make a comparison with Switzerland is an overstatement,
but the attractions of the region's contours with no hill
higher than 365m (1,200ft) are varied and impressive.

The nearest train stations to Clécy (*see page* 78) are at
Caen and Flers. There are bus services connecting Caen,
Thury-Harcourt, Clécy, Condé-sur-Noireau and Flers.

Sights

Starting out from Mont St-Michel (*see page* 73) head first
for **Villedieu-les-Poêles** (pop. 4,300) via Avranches (*see
page 74*). This typically Norman town enjoys a reputation
as a centre of the metalworking trade. A quick stroll
through the narrow streets will provide a clear indication
of the type of goods produced here: saucepans, frying pans,
kettles – all made of copper. Most of these items, which
are mainly of decorative value, are made at the **Atelier du
Cuivre** (54 rue du Général-Huard, tel: 02 33 51 31 85, fax:
02 33 51 04 96; weekdays 9am–noon, 2–5pm). Perhaps
of greater interest is the local bell-foundry which continues to use the traditional methods. The ★ **Fonderie de
Cloches** (10 Rue du Pont Chignon, tel: 02 33 61 00 56,

Villedieu-les-Poêles

77

Copper is a local speciality

Tour de l'Horloge in Vire

fax: 02 33 90 02 99; open Tuesday to Saturday 8am–noon, 1.30–5.30pm; mid-June–mid-September daily – please phone first if intending to visit on Sunday and Monday between September and June) makes bells of all sizes in its old workshop. Many are exported through the world. The nearby church of **Notre-Dame**, not far from the foundry, dates from the 15th century and is admired for its impressive late Gothic style.

The symbol of **Vire** (pop. 15,000) is the **Tour de l'Horloge** in the town centre. The lower section dates from the 13th century and a belltower was added some 200 years later. The tower is one of the few old buildings in the town which survived World War II unscathed. In a loop on the River Vire and accessible from the Place du Château stand the ruins of a **keep**. It was built in 1123 by Henri I Beauclerc and affords a fine view over the valley. The town grew up on a textile industry and its bawdy workers' songs were called *Vaux de Vire*, said to be the origin of the word 'Vauderville'.

A detour to **La-Ferrière-Harang** about 20km (12 miles) north of Vire will reward those with a dare-devil streak. The bridge over the River Soulevre claims to be the original European bungee-jumping centre, started by a New Zealander, and it remains a favourite launching pad for fearless jumpers.

Clécy, on the other hand, the 'capital' of Swiss Normandy, offers other more orthodox sporting activities. Brightly-coloured canoes and kayaks can often be seen on the stretch of river between Clécy and Pont d'Ouilly. As well as plenty of short walks two long-distance routes pass nearby: GR36 Ouistreham to Ecouché (145km/90 miles) and GR221 Pont d'Ouilly to Bény-Bocage (52km/32 miles). Other activities include: riding, hang-gliding in St-Omer, golf, sailing, flying, gliding, climbing and fishing.

A day-long tour of the region starting from Clécy is signposted as the **Route de la Suisse Normande**, but historic buildings, picturesque town centres or interesting museums are in short supply – the distinguishing features of the tour are the rustic charm and peaceful countryside. At **St-Rémy** the route leaves behind the narrow Orne Valley and winds its way up the sun-bathed hillsides to the **Route des Crêtes**. The Crests' Road heads east over the undulating plain to **St-Omer**, the only place where other traffic may slow progress. Above the cliffs at **Rochers de la Houle** nature has created a perfect take-off point for hang-gliders.

Thury-Harcourt (pop. 1,800) is the northern gate to Swiss Normandy and, like Clécy, it has in recent years become a busy tourist centre with hotels, bars and shops. The

Try some bungee-jumping

Enjoying an aerial view

town's name derives from the Harcourts who built their family residence here at the beginning of the 18th century. The duke's castle was burnt down in 1944 with only the ruins now left standing in splendid parkland. On summer days it is pleasant to make the 5-km (3-mile) walk through the grounds. At the northern edge of the town the Orne loops round cutting between steep rocks to create the **Boucle du Hom** and walkers can follow a path along the banks of the river here. The main road to Caen leaves the river valley in the town and Caen lies 26km (16 miles) to the northeast.

For a pleasant detour sweeping round the Orne Valley in an arc, start in the west at **Mont-Pinçon** (365m/1,200ft), the region's highest peak. Near a lake fed by the River Druance stands the 16th-century **Château de Pontécoulant** and the Musée Départementale.

Admiral Dumont d'Urville was a famous son of the little town of **Condé-sur-Noireau**. He was born in 1790 and among the most famous of his exploits was the well-documented exploration of lands in the South Pacific including New Guinea, New Zealand and the Antarctic. A memorial to the seafarer stands in the town's Place de l' Hôtel de Ville. The stones at the foot of the monument were brought back from the Antarctic by a fellow explorer.

Follow the river Noireau as far as the small, picturesque town, **Pont d'Ouilly** on the River Orne, now one of Suisse Normande's principal resorts. Although rebuilt and modernised after the war, along the valley there is evidence of an earlier age when spinning and tanning were the local industries. Return to Clécy via **Le Bô**.

Boucle du Hom

79

Château de Pontécoulant and interior detail

Art History

Normandy's genius has shaped French and even world culture, in three areas – architecture, literature and art.

Architecture

During the first one thousand years of modern times the architecture of Normandy was influenced chiefly by the Romans and then the Scandinavian Vikings, but from the middle of the 11th century, a distinctly independent style evolved. Admittedly, early Romanesque influences of the Burgundian school were adopted, but a distinctive Norman style soon emerged. Fine examples exist in the Romanesque abbey at Jumièges Monastery as well as the Romanesque galleried basilica at the Church of St-Etienne in Caen. Rounded arches in the interior; a gallery with openings to the central nave; a facade with twin towers and a tower above the crossing on a rectangular ground plan. These were to become the typical features of Norman style – a style which was even 'exported' abroad. London's Westminster Abbey, built between 1050 and 1065 by Edward the Confessor, still serves to illustrate the talents of the architect, who had, in fact, spent some time in exile in Normandy. One of the most striking features of Norman architecture is the fact that the strict rules for building in stone that had applied until then were cast aside. Thick, solid walls which had previously borne the weight of the roof were replaced by buttresses – allowing the entry of light – and ribbed vaults, two features which pointed clearly towards the next development of the style into Gothic.

Slender columns are typical Gothic features

The first Gothic building was the Eglise St-Denis in Ile de France built by Abbot Suger in the middle of the 12th century. This style soon spread throughout Europe. And yet certain elements, such as the lantern tower above the crossing, were unique to Normandy. One such example is the lantern tower, apparently made of engraved stone, in Coutances Cathedral. Even during the Romanesque period architects sought to allow as much daylight as possible through the crossing tower to illuminate the otherwise gloomy interior and they often placed the altar at a focal point for daylight. During the Gothic era many major sacred buildings were built in Normandy and the decorations became even more ornate, culminating in the extravagant late Gothic Flamboyant style. Notre-Dame Cathedral and the St-Ouen Church in Rouen are superb examples, as is the Church of Notre-Dame in Pont-de-l'Arche.

The French term 'flamboyant' means 'flaming', as the tracery of the bays and rose windows are said to resemble flickering flames.

Flamboyant style in St-Ouen

Rouen Cathedral by Monet

Claude Monet House

Painting

Théodore Géricault (1791–1824) was one of the first native Norman artists and sculptors. Born in Rouen he was an important influence on French Romantic art. He began his career copying old masters such as Rubens and Titian, but his unorthodox approach and bold use of colour incurred the disapproval of his teacher. He first came to the public's attention with an exhibition piece entitled *Officer of Light Horse* at the Salon of 1812. Seven years later he produced his masterpiece *The Raft of Medusa*, based on a shipwreck which had just caused a sensation in France. Towards the end of his life he painted five portraits of the insane.

In the year Géricault died, Eugène Boudin (1824–98) was born in Honfleur. His best known works are seascapes, including *Deauville* and *Harbour of Trouville*. He was a precursor of the Impressionist movement, which started in the 1860s, reaching its climax between 1870 and 1880. The best known exponents of Impressionism include Claude Monet, Camille Pissarro, Auguste Renoir, Alfred Sisley, Jean Frédéric Bazille (1841–1870) and, at times, Edgar Degas and Paul Cézanne.

It was Claude Monet (1840–1926) who provided the impetus for this celebrated movement. His family moved from Paris to Le Havre when he was eight and there he met Eugène Boudin, who encouraged him to paint in the open air. One day he painted a picture of the harbour, *Impression: Soleil Levant*. When he exhibited in Paris in 1874 it gained one critic's derision as *Impressioniste*. He met Camille Pissarro while studying in Paris, and a few years later he became acquainted with Renoir, Sisley and Bazille and they worked together. The aim of this circle of artists was to convey on canvas the nuances, as they saw them, of natural colour and light.

Monet settled at Giverny near Vernon in 1883. The country house with a garden that he laid out himself was to be his home until he died more then 40 years later. Occasionally he made excursions into the nearby countryside and even to London and Venice. Portrayed in the changing intensity of daylight, *Rouen Cathedral* (1894) is one of his most famous works. During the later years of his life, however, he rarely ventured outside his own magnificent garden where he loved painting the colourful flowerbeds and the water-lily pond.

While Monet was a Norman only by choice, native Norman painters include Raoul Dufy (1877–1953) and Emile Othon Friesz (1879–1949), both of whom came from Le Havre. Fernand Léger (1881–1955) was a native of Argentan. Camille Pissarro (1830–1903) and Georges Braque (1882–1963), the master of Cubism, both ended their days in Normandy.

Literature

In the Middle Ages it became possible to talk of Norman literature. Writers emerged at both the Duke of Normandy's court and in the many monasteries, which had developed from the 7th century onwards as religious and spiritual centres. This early literature dealt primarily with historical themes. The Jumièges monk, Guillaume Caillouwie, wrote *The History of the Vikings* and Guillaume de Poitiers, the archdeacon of Lisieux, wrote a discourse in Latin on William II, Duke of Normandy and King of England. Also using Latin, Guy de Ponthieu documented the famous Battle of Hastings in 1066.

In the early 13th century when Normandy and France united the region began to lose some of its identity, but in the ensuing centuries it was nevertheless home to many world famous writers. One of France's greatest playwrights, Pierre Corneille (1606–84) was born in Rouen and, having worked initially as a lawyer for the king, published his first comedy at the age of 23. After the tremendous success of his first work, in 1637 he published the tragi-comedy *El Cid* – a controversial play, and one of the most important works of the 17th century.

Gustave Flaubert, born in Rouen in 1821, ranks as one of Normandy's literary masters. The son of a doctor, he reluctantly studied law at Paris, where his friendship with Maxime du Camp, Victor Hugo, and Louise Colet who became his lover, stimulated his already apparent talent for writing. Soon after finishing his studies, he was afflicted by a nervous disease which may have been partly responsible for the morbidity and pessimism revealed in his first masterpiece, *Madame Bovary*, the tale of a bourgeois

83

Flaubert

Madame Bovary Museum in Ry

romantic tragedy. After its publication in 1857, Flaubert was accused of offending public morality but was later acquitted. In his writings Flaubert fought against the use of banal everyday language, against clichés and platitudes, resisting attempts to debase the French language.

Flaubert enjoyed a close friendship with the third great Norman writer, Guy de Maupassant (1850–93). He came from near Fécamp and worked for several years as a government clerk but encouraged by Flaubert he took to writing. Early lyrical and dramatic works were overshadowed by his first success, *Boule de Suif*, in 1880, which was then followed by a highly productive decade. He wrote six novels, numerous travel guides and about 260 short stories before he fell victim to syphilis in 1892 and died two years later in Paris.

Another Norman who achieved fame for his writings was Alexis de Tocqueville (1805–59), who specialised in the realm of historical and political analysis. A man of aristocratic background from the north of the Cotentin Peninsula, he travelled to the USA and made a study of the American political system. His shrewd conclusions, published in 1835 as *De la Démocratie en Amérique*, quickly established his reputation. He later became active in politics, reaching the post of French foreign minister. Having dedicated the last years of his life to writing historical and political works he died in Cannes in 1859.

Among other French writers who found inspiration on the Normandy coast, Marcel Proust (1871–1922) is probably the best known. He was a frequent visitor to the coastal resorts and for health reasons, between 1881 and 1893, he spent many weeks taking the sea air.

Alexis de Tocqueville

Festivals

Jan/February	Fair in Caen.
February	Carnival in Caen.
March	Sausage market in Mortagne-au-Perche.
April	Antiques market in L'Aigle.
May	Jazz under the Apple Trees Festival in Coutances; international hockey tournament in Deauville with regatta on the English Channel; Normandy festival in Etretat; Joan of Arc festival in Rouen; seaman's festival in Honfleur; international regatta in Cherbourg; annual flower festival in Beuvron-en-Auge.
June	Sea Festival in Le Havre; Anniversary of Normandy Landings on D-Day Beaches; Eure summer festival begins; Pilgrimage on Trinity Sunday in Fécamp.
July	Jazz festival and horse-racing in Deauville; Granville Sea Festival; pilgrimage to Mont St-Michel; festival of classical music in Honfleur; jazz festival in Trouville; fireworks in Lisieux; bridge tournament in Deauville; pilgrimage to Mont St-Michel; Camembert-Fair.
August	Polo world championship in Deauville; 'La Fanatic Cup' windsurfing competition in Cabourg; festival of the sea in St-Vaast-la-Hougue; pilgrimage in Lisieux; son-et-lumière in Forges-les-Eaux; Cheese Fair in Livarot.
September	Festival of Ste Thérèse in Lisieux; Sea Festival in Le Havre; American film festival in Deauville; international hang-gliding convention in Dieppe; St Michael's pilgrimage at Mont St-Michel; Neufchâtel- en-Bray Cheese Festival ; Music Festival in Orne – three week programme of baroque, opera, chamber, jazz and dance music performed in abbeys and châteaux.
October	Vintage car rally in Deauville; horse-racing and parade in Haras-du-Pin; apple fair in Vimoutiers; Festival of the Shrimp in Honfleur.
November	Herring fair in Lieurey and in Dieppe; cider festival in Beuvron-en-Auge; St-Romain fair in Rouen; St-Martin fair in Neufchâtel-en-Bray.
December	Turkey festival in Sées; St Nicholas market in Evreux.

Joan of Arc

Mont St-Michel

85

Hang-gliding Convention

Food and Drink

Take a stroll through one of Normandy's many weekly markets, but be ready to exercise a little self-control. The appetising selection of cheese, fish, vegetables and meat will certainly arouse your taste buds, but the visual effect can be quite stunning too. Regard these markets as a challenge – many of the delights on offer will be hard to resist.

Livarot cheese

Norman cuisine takes no account of calorie charts. Butter, cream and Calvados have a permanent place next to the cooker. Double cream, sometimes even triple cream, is often used to enrich sauces.

The fishing tradition ensures that menus can include turbot, skate, monkfish, sole, carp, sea trout and salmon. Seafood is also plentiful with crabs, scallops, mussels, prawns and oysters often served together as *fruits de mer*. On the Cotentin Peninsula in particular, the custom of dripping a little lemon juice on to oysters is frowned upon. Instead, in St-Vaast and elsewhere, the precious molluscs are served with a shallot and apple vinegar sauce. For those who prefer their seafood cooked, try *Huîtres aux Pommes*. The shelled oysters are served *au gratin* on slightly sour apples. *Marmite Dieppoise* is a fish soup cooked in the Dieppe style with a creamy sauce.

Abundance of seafood

87

But fish and seafood are not the only main courses. *Agneau Pré-salé* is often found and is a dish made from lambs, which have been fed on the grass of the salty meadows along the Normandy coast. Offal dishes such as *Tripes à la mode de Caen* are also popular. *Soupe à la Graisse* (dripping soup) consists of several types of vegetables, including leek, cabbage, green beans, celery and parsley, cooked with plenty of dripping.

The symbol of the *département* of Calvados is, of course, the world renowned apple brandy which bears the same name. The famous *trou Normand* refers to a glass of Calvados taken during the meal, creating a *trou* or hole for more feasting. The ratio between sweet and sour apples for the unfermented juice is kept a well-guarded secret. The juice can be described as *cidre bouché* when an alcohol content of 5 percent is reached and this type of apple wine, which can be bought in bottles, is served throughout Normandy. The unfermented juice which is made into Calvados stays in the barrel on its yeast for two years, and it is then distilled in stages until an alcohol content of 25 percent is attained. Storage in oak casks gives what would otherwise be a colourless liquid an amber tint. Calvados which is two years old is described as *vieux*, after three years, the producer may call it *vieille réserve* and after six years *hors d'âge*. Other liquid delights include *Pommeau*, an 18 percent apple liqueur and *Bénédictine*, a herb-flavoured liqueur from Fécamp.

Calvados in oak casks

Restaurant selection

The following is a selection of recommended restaurants in Normandy's major centres.

The restaurants below are listed according to four categories: €€€€ – very expensive; €€€ – expensive; €€ – moderate and € – inexpensive. (€ is €25 or less per person; €€ = €25–40; €€€ = €40–60; €€€€ = more than €60)

Avranches: Croix d'Or, 83 rue de la Constitution, tel: 02 33 58 04 88, fax: 02 33 58 06 95. Closed January and Sunday evening during winter. This hotel is home to the best restaurant in Avranches. €€

Bayeux: Le Lion d'Or, 71 rue St-Jean, tel: 02 31 92 06 90. Closed mid-December to mid-January and Saturday and Monday lunch. The best Norman cuisine in town in this hotel's restaurant. Speciality of the house is a type of black pudding, *andouille*. €€–€€€. **Le Petit Normand**, 35 rue Larcher, tel: 02 31 22 88 66. Closed Thursday during winter and January. Classic Norman dishes feature in this 16th century establishment close to the Cathedral. Specialities include seafood and local cider. €€

Charcuterie delights, Bayeux

88

Cabourg: Le Beau Site, 30 avenue Foch, tel: 02 31 24 42 88. There is a beautiful view of the sea from the terrace of this fish and seafood restaurant. Specialities include *Crabe Farçi* (stuffed crab) lobster and mussels. €€€. **Hostellerie Guillaume le Conquérant**, 2 rue d'Hastings in neighbouring Dives-sur-Mer, tel: 02 31 91 07 26. A 16th-century coach house, part of which is now a traditional-style restaurant. €€–€€€

Caen: La Bourride, 15 rue du Vaugueux, tel: 02 31 93 50 76, fax: 02 31 93 29 63. Closed mid-August to early September. Atmospheric and highly rated restaurant – probably Caen's best with two Michelin stars. One of their specialities is called 'Symphony around an Apple' – it tastes as good as it sounds. €€€€. **Le Dauphin**, 29 rue Gémare, tel: 02 31 86 22 26, fax: 02 31 86 35 14. Closed mid-July to early August. An exquisitely furnished former monastery offering local specialities. €€–€€€

Cherbourg: some restaurants in Cherbourg produce good-quality regional specialities at reasonable prices. **Le Grandgousier**, 21 rue de l'Abbaye, tel: 02 33 53 19 43. Closed Saturday lunch and Sunday dinner. Excellent seafood restaurant, which, although located away from the centre of town, is worth the detour for a memorable gastronomic experience. €€€. **Café de Paris**, 40 Quai Caligny, tel: 02 33 43 12 36, fax: 02 33 43 98 49. Closed Sunday evening and Monday in winter. Everything from giant-sized 'assiettes de fruits de mer' to very reasonable set menus, where the accent is on the freshest of fish. €€–€€€

Deauville: Le Ciro's, Boulevard de la Mer, tel: 02 31 14 31 31, fax: 02 31 98 66 71. Closed Tuesday and Wednesday, October to May. Deauville's undisputed gastronomic citadel, situated on the promenade. Popular with celebrities. €€€–€€€€. **Le Spinnaker**, 52 rue Mirabeau, tel: 02 31 88 24 40, fax: 02 31 88 43 58. Closed Tuesday in winter; Monday and period in November. Top-quality fish and seafood restaurant. Traditional Norman cuisine with generous use of cider and Calvados. €€–€€€

Dieppe: Marmite Dieppoise, 8 rue St-Jean, tel: 02 35 84 24 26. Closed Thursday evening, Monday and 1 November to 31 March. One of the house specialities is the famous local dish, bowls of shellfish and whitefish, after which the restaurant is named. €€–€€€. **Les Écamias**, 129 quai Henri 1V, tel: 02 35 84 67 67. Closed Monday. Good, fresh seafood features in this traditional, small restaurant. Specialities include 'moules marinières'. €–€€

Étretat: Les Roches Blanches, terrasse Boudin, tel: 02 35 27 07 34. Traditional Normandy cuisine, specialising in seafood, served in this pleasing seafront restaurant. €€€

Evreux: Hôtel-Restaurant de France, 29 rue St-Thomas, tel: 02 32 39 09 25. Best establishment in the town with attractive garden by the River Iton. €€€. **Le Jardin d'Élodie**, 11 rue de la Harpe, tel: 02 32 38 08 66. Closed Monday in winter. Splendid view of the cathedral. In a spacious setting, this restaurant caters for all tastes – from carnivores to fish lovers. €€

Gothic setting in Evreux

Forges-les-Eaux: Auberge du Beau Lieu, on the D915, Route Gournay, tel: 02 35 90 50 36, fax: 02 35 90 35 98. Closed Monday evening, Wednesday lunch and Tuesday. Norman specialities served *al fresco*. €€–€€€. **Hôtel de la Paix**, 15 rue Neufchâtel, tel: 02 35 90 51 22, fax: 02 35 09 83 62. Closed Sunday evening out of season and Monday lunchtime. Tourist menus at reasonable prices. €–€€

Granville: La Gentilhommière, 152 rue Couraye, tel: 02 33 50 17 99. Closed Sunday dinner, Monday in winter and early March. Specialities include a stew made with Iles Chausey lobster. €€€. **Normandy Chaumière**, 20 rue Paul-Poirier, tel: 02 33 50 01 71, fax: 02 33 50 15 34. Option of eating *al fresco*. Good value shellfish menu. €€–€€€

Al fresco in Honfleur

Honfleur: Au Vieux Honfleur, 13 Quai St Étienne, tel: 02 31 89 15 31. Closed January. Must book. Popular, attractive establishment. Specialising in the freshest seafood. **€€€**. **L'Absinthe**, 10 quai de la Quarantaine, tel: 02 31 89 39 00, fax: 02 31 89 53 60. Closed mid-November to mid-December. Excellent cuisine with a choice of menus, culminating in a seven course menu gourmand. **€€€**

Le Havre: Villa du Havre, Rue Guy de Maupassant, tel: 02 35 46 27 32, fax: 02 35 54 78 81. Closed Sunday evening and Wednesday evening and Monday. A beautiful 19th century house, recently restored to a high standard, complementing the haute cuisine. **€€€–€€€€**

Le Tréport: Le Homard Bleu, 45 quai François 1er, tel: 02 35 86 15 89, fax: 02 35 86 49 21. Seafood restaurant located along the harbour quay with good value menus. **€€**. **St Louis**, 43 Quai François 1er, tel: 02 35 86 20 70, fax: 02 35 50 67 10. Closed 20 November to 20 December. Bustling atmosphere in this quayside restaurant. **€€**

Les Andelys: La Chaîne d'Or, 27 rue Grande, tel: 02 32 54 00 31, fax: 02 32 54 05 68. Closed Sunday evening, Tuesday lunch and Monday. Restaurant offering excellent Norman cuisine in an 18th-century *auberge*. **€€€**

Lisieux: Ferme du Roy, about 2km (1¼ miles) from the town on the road to Deauville, tel: 02 31 31 33 98. Best restaurant in the area set in an old farmhouse. **Aux Acacias**, 13 rue Résistance, tel: 02 31 62 10 95, fax: 02 31 32 59 06. Closed Sunday evening, Monday (except holidays) and Thursday evening in winter. Traditional Norman cuisine. Central location. **€€–€€€**

Coffee-time in Rouen's Vieux-Marché

Mont St-Michel: La Mère Poulard, Grande rue, tel: 02 33 60 14 01. Norman specialities in this famous restaurant. The fluffy omelettes are sublime. **€€€–€€€€**

Rouen: Gill, 9 quai Bourse, tel: 02 35 71 16 14, fax: 02 35 71 96 91. Closed Sunday and Monday. Rouen's best restaurant, holding two Michelin stars. Specialities include puff pastry dishes or pigeon. **€€€€**. **Les Nymphéas**, 9 rue de la Pie, tel: 02 35 89 26 69, fax: 02 35 70 98 81. Closed Sunday evening, Tuesday lunch and Monday. A superb restaurant specialising in both meat and fish. One Michelin star. **€€€–€€€€**

Vernon: Restaurant Les Fleurs, 71 rue Carnot, tel: 02 32 51 16 80, fax: 02 32 21 30 51. Closed Sunday evening and Monday. Excellent regional cuisine. Must book as there are a limited number of covers. **€€**

Activity Holidays

A coastal location and open countryside make Normandy an ideal region for an activity holiday, especially those in or on the water. **Windsurfers** will inevitably make for those parts of the coast where the weather conditions are most favourable. The west coast of the Cotentin Peninsula: Kairon Plage, Plage de la Potinière near Barneville-Carteret, Le Rozel, Siouville. The north coast of the Cotentin Peninsula: Urville-Nacqueville. Calvados: Côte Fleurie (windsurfing is sometimes restricted at busy times). Côte d'Albâtre: Cap d'Antifer, Etretat, Ste-Marguerite, Mer-les-Bains near Le Tréport.

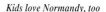

Utah Beach

Utah Beach on the east coast of the Cotentin Peninsula has developed into a popular place for **sand yachting** as the flat beach and prevailing wind direction provide the right conditions for the sport. All the equipment can be hired locally (Camping Le Cormoran, Ravenoville/Ste-Mère-Eglise, tel: 02 33 41 33 94, beginning of April to the end of September). There about 50 **sailing clubs** on the coast which hire out sailing boats (eg École de Voile, Barneville-Carteret, tel: 02 33 04 83 54; Port Chentereyne, Cherbourg, tel: 02 33 94 28 05; École de Voile, Place Napoléon, Cherbourg, tel: 02 33 94 13 73; Yacht Club, Granville, tel: 02 33 50 04 25; Centre Régional de Nautisme, Granville, tel: 02 33 50 18 95).

91

Marina in Deauville

As Normandy, in particular the Pays d'Auge, has a tradition of horse-breeding, **riding** is a popular pastime. Information on riding centres is available on tel: 02 31 79 23 05 and from local tourist offices. There are several companies in the region which organise horse riding and rides in horse-drawn carriages. Contact: Ferme de Loisir, 76440 Mauquenchy, Pays de Bray, tel: 02 35 90 58 22, fax: 02 35 90 49 46. Brochures are available from Comité Régional de Tourisme de Normandie, 14 rue Charles Corbeau, F-27000 Evreux, tel: 02 32 33 79 00, fax: 02 32 31 19 04.

Kids love Normandy, too

A **cruise** on the Seine can add to the pleasure of a visit. Boats ply between Paris and Honfleur and passengers can leave or join at any of the intervening places. For more details contact Fleuves et Loisirs, 29 avenue Claude Monet, F-95510 Vetheuil, tel: 02 34 78 16 32, fax: 02 34 78 23 96. 'Le Normandie', a 53-berth hotel ship, takes six nights/seven days to cover the same route. Contact: Aqua Viva, quai de Grenelle, F-75015, tel: 02 45 75 52 60, fax: 02 45 75 52 31. Boat trips between Le Havre and Rouen (lunch included) are organised by 'Salamandre', M Fortin, BP 1086, F-76062 Le Havre, Cedex, tel: 02 35 42 01 31.

The area southwest of Alençon is one where **ramblers** will find some splendid walks. For more details contact Maison du Parc, Parc Régional Normandie-Maine, F-61320 Carrouges, tel: 02 33 27 21 15.

WEST

Getting There

By plane

Air France flies direct to Paris from London and New York and other US cities. Travellers from America, however, may find it cheaper to take a charter flight to London, then go onward from there. Air France operates a rail package with flights available from a number of UK airports to Paris, then onward by train to the region. These inclusive tickets can also be combined with a rail pass. Brit Air offer services from Gatwick to Caen and Le Havre, bookable through Air France. Régional Airlines offer flights from Gatwick to Rouen, also bookable through Air France. There are five airports in Normandy with international connections – Caen, Cherbourg, Deauville, Le Havre and Rouen. Several low-cost carriers serve these airports.

In the UK: Air France, 100 Hammersmith Road, London W6 7JP, tel: 0845 0845 111; www.airfrance.com/uk

In the US: Air France, 666 Fifth Avenue, New York NY 10019, tel: 212 315 1122 (toll-free reservations: 1 800 237 2747); 850l Wilshire Boulevard, Beverly Hills, Los Angeles, CA 90211, tel: 213 688 9220.

The docks at Cherbourg

By ship

Several ferry and high-speed jetfoil services operate across the English Channel from the UK, Ireland and the Channel Islands to Normandy. All carry cars and foot passengers.

Brittany Ferries offer sailings from Portsmouth to Caen (up to three sailings daily), Portsmouth to St Malo (one daily sailing) and a slightly cheaper 'Les Routiers' service from Poole to Cherbourg (summer only). For details contact: The Brittany Centre, Wharf Road, Portsmouth PO2 8RU; or from Millbay Docks, Plymouth PL1 3EW. Central reservations, tel: 08703 665 333; www.brittanyferries.com

P & O European Ferries sail from Portsmouth to Cherbourg (up to six sailings a day; summer only fast ferry service, up to three sailings a day) and Le Havre, and also operate the short sea route from Dover to Calais. Contact: P & O, Channel House, Channel View Road, Dover CT17 9TJ, tel: 0870 600 0611; www.poferries.com

Condor Ferries operate between Portsmouth and Poole and Cherbourg. Contact: Condor Head Office, New Harbour Road South, Hamworthy, Poole, Dorset BH15 4AJ, tel: 01202 207207. Central bookings, tel: 0845 345 2000 or visit the website on www.condorferries.co.uk

By train

Eurostar rail services between London (Waterloo), Lille and Paris (Gare du Nord) is a very fast and frequent service. France has a fast and efficient rail network operated

Trains connect all the main cities

NON GARDE

by the SNCF (Société Nationale des Chemins de Fer de France). There are direct connections to the main cities of the region from Paris Saint-Lazare and Montparnasse stations. Paris to Rouen takes 1 hour 20 minutes, Paris-Caen 3 hours, Paris-Cherbourg 4 hours, Paris-Deauville 2 hours (for further details of rail connections, *see Places*).

Tickets may be booked for through journeys from outside France. In the UK tickets can be booked from any British Rail station, including ferry and Channel Tunnel travel. There are several rail-only and rail combination passes available to foreign visitors. These must be bought before departing for France. In the UK a Eurodomino Pass offers unlimited rail travel on any 3, 5 or 10 days within a month. Visitors from North America have a wider choice, starting with the basic France Railpass which offers four or nine days' unlimited travel within a month.

Then there are various types of Eurail Pass which offer varying periods of first-class travel throughout Europe; the Eurail Youthpass offers a similar deal for young people under 26. The France Rail 'n' Drive Pass offers a flexible rail and car rental package, while the Fly Rail 'n' Drive Pass combines internal flights on Air Inter with train travel and car hire.

In the UK information and reservations for all the above services can be obtained from Rail Europe, 179 Piccadilly, London W1 0BA, tel: 08705 848 848 or visit www.raileurope.co.uk **In the US** contact Raileurope Inc. on their nationwide toll-free number 1 800 4 EURAIL or in **Canada** 1 800 361 7425.

By car
Normandy is an ideal destination for car travellers, with good motorways from Paris (N13 to Evreux and Caen, N14 to Rouen). The roads are reasonably uncrowded, except on the main routes to and from Paris at peak holiday times (the first and last weekends in August). Almost all motorways in France are privately owned and subject to tolls (credit cards are usually accepted). A toll is also payable on the Brotonne Bridge and the Tancarville Bridge over the Seine, as well as the Pont de Normandie, the impressive motorway bridge connecting Le Havre to Honfleur, which has improved access from the port to the coastal resorts of Deauville, Trouville etc. Caen centre is less than 30 minutes from the port of Ouistreham and Rouen is only about an hour away from the ports of Le Havre or Dieppe.

Journey's end

Le Shuttle, the Channel Tunnel service taking cars and their passengers from Folkestone to Calais on a drive-on-drive-off system, takes 35 minutes. There are two trains an hour, rising to four trains during peak periods. Contact, tel: 08705 35 35 35 or visit www.eurotunnel.com

Getting Around

By train

Information on services is available from stations (*gare* SCNF) and from Rail Europe Travel Centre at 178 Piccadilly, London W1J 9AL, tel: 08705 848 848 or visit www.raileurope.co.uk. If you intend to travel extensively by train it may be worth obtaining a rail pass before leaving home (*see page 93*). Children under 4 travel free, from 4 to 12 for half-fare.

Train et Vélo: Bicycles can be hired from most main stations. On many trains, cycles can be transported free of charge in the luggage van. Free brochures on transporting cycles by train are available at all French stations.

By car

British, US, Canadian and Australian licences are all valid in France and you should always carry your vehicle's registration document and insurance (third party is the absolute minimum, and a green card is strongly recommended). The Automobile Club National will assist any motorist whose own club has an agreement with it. Contact them at 9 rue Anatole-de-la-Forge, 75017 Paris, tel: 01 42 27 82 00, fax: 01 40 53 90 52.

Britons must remember to drive on the right and that priority on French roads is always given to vehicles approaching from the right. The minimum age for driving in France is 18; foreigners are not permitted to drive on a provisional licence. The use of seat belts and crash helmets for motorcyclists is compulsory. Children under 10 are not permitted to ride in the front seat unless fitted with a rear-facing safety seat, or if the car has no rear seat.

Speed limits are as follows, unless otherwise indicated: 80 mph (130 kph) on toll motorways; 68 mph (110 kph) on other motorways and dual carriageways; 56 mph (90 kph) on other roads except in towns where the limit is 30 mph (50 kph). There is a *minimum* speed limit of 50 mph (80 kph) on the outside lane of motorways during daylight with good visibility and on level ground. In an accident or emergency, call the police (dial 17) or use the free emergency telephones on motorways.

Car hire

Some fly/drive deals work out reasonably well on short visits. French Railways offer a good deal on their combined train/car rental bookings. Weekly rates often work out better than a daily hire. Most companies will not hire to anyone under 23, or 21 if paying by credit card and the hirer must have held a full licence for at least a year. The major car hire companies have local offices in Normandy's main cities.

Discussing itineraries

In towns the speed limit is 50 kmph

95

Weekly rates work out cheaper than daily hire

Facts for the Visitor

Visas

All visitors to France need a valid passport. No visa is currently required by visitors from any EU country or from the US, Canada or Japan. Nationals of other countries do require a visa. If in any doubt check with the French consulate in your country.

Enjoying the summer

Tourist information

The French Tourist Board can supply information and brochures on all regions of France (www.franceguide.com).

In the UK: Maison de la France/French Government Tourist Office, 178 Piccadilly, London W1V 0AL, tel: 090 68 244123 (60 pence per minute), fax: 020 7493 6594. Normandy Tourist Board, The Old Bakery, Bath Hill, Keynsham, Bristol BS18 1HG, tel: 0117 986 0386, fax: 0117 986 0379.

In the US: Maison de la France/French Government Tourist Office, 444 Madison Avenue, 16th Floor, New York NY 10022-6903, tel: 410-282 8310, fax: 410-212 838; 9454 Wilshire Boulevard, Suite 715, Beverley Hills, Los Angeles CA 90212-2967, tel: 310-271 6665; 645 North Michigan Avenue, Suite 630, Chicago, Illinois 606ll-2836, tel: 312-337 6301.

In Paris: Maison de la France, 8 Avenue de l'Opéra, 75001 Paris, tel: 01 42 96 10 23.

In Normandy: Comité Régional de Tourisme de Normandie, 14 rue Charles Corbeau, F-27000 Evreux, tel: 02 32 33 79 00, fax: 02 32 31 19 04.

Dieppe Tourist Office

Rouen Tourist Office

The following tourist offices are in the main towns covered in the Places section of this guide and can usually provide information about their region: **Caen**, Office du Tourisme, 14 place St-Pierre, tel: 02 31 27 14 10, fax: 02 31 27 14 13; Calvados Tourisme, Place du Canada, F-14000 Caen, tel: 02 31 27 90 30, fax: 02 31 27 90 35; **Cherbourg**, Office du Tourisme, 50100 Cherbourg-Octeville, 2 quai Alexandre III, tel: 02 33 93 52 02; **Dieppe**, Syndicat d'Initiative, Pont Jehan Ango, 76204 Dieppe, tel: 02 32 14 40 60, fax: 02 32 14 40 61, closed Sunday. Information kiosk, Rotonde de la Plage, July and August only, tel: 02 35 84 28 70; **Evreux**, Office du Tourisme, Place du Général de Gaulle, 27000, tel: 02 32 24 04 43, fax: 02 32 31 28 45; Comité Départemental de Tourisme de l'Eure, Hôtel du Département, Boulevard G. Chavin, tel: 32 31 51 51, fax: 02 32 31 05 98; **Le Havre**, Syndicat d'Initiative, 186 Boulevard Clémenceau, BP 649, 76059 Le Havre, tel: 02 32 74 04 04, fax: 02 35 42 38 39; **Rouen**, Syndicat d'Initiative, 25 place de la Cathédrale, 76000, tel: 02 32 08 32 40, fax: 02 32 08 32 44. Open Easter to end of October, Monday to Saturday 9am–7pm, Sunday

9am–7pm, Sunday and holidays 9.30am–12.30pm, 2.30–6pm; November to Easter, daily 9am–6.30pm, closed Sunday; **Suisse Normande**, Office du Tourisme, Place de l'Eglise, F-14570 Clécy, tel: 02 31 69 79 95; Office du Tourisme, Place de la Mairie, Condé-sur-Noir, tel: 02 31 69 27 64; Office du Tourisme, Place St-Sauveur, 14220 Thury-Harcourt, tel: 02 31 79 70 45, fax: 02 31 79 15 42.

Currency and exchange

The main unit of currency is the euro, which is divided into 100 cents (c). Coins are in denominations of 1 and 2 euros; 1, 2, 5, 20 and 50 cents. Notes are available in the following denominations 5, 10, 20, 50, 100, 200 and 500 euros.

By using a credit card, cash can be withdrawn from automatic teller machines outside normal banking hours. Eurocheques are no longer accepted.

Try to use up any notes or coins before leaving, as converting back to sterling or dollars can prove expensive as some banks may make a charge for this service. In the UK, banks will be able to change notes, but not coins. If possible, take travellers' cheques.

Cash point

If you need more information about the euro get in touch with your bank or consult the travel pages of the Foreign Office website on www.fco.gov.uk

Credit cards are accepted in most hotels. Paying with plastic cards may be a problem in the remoter rural regions.

Tipping

In restaurants and cafés a service charge is always included in the price, but an additional tip is usually expected.

Opening times

There are no strict regulations for shop opening hours in France. In general, shops and banks in country areas stay open for shorter periods than branches in town.
Banks
9am–12noon and 2–4pm, closed Saturday and Monday.
Shops
Shops are normally open 8am–12noon and 2–7pm. Many of the hypermarkets are open 9am–9pm, but they often open later on Monday at either noon or 1pm.
Official Offices
Monday to Friday, 9am–12noon and 2–5pm.
Post Offices
The PTT Post Offices (*Administration des Postes Télégraphes et Téléphones*) and P et T (*Ministère des Postes et Télécommunications*) are open from Monday to Friday 9am–7pm (in country areas Monday to Friday 8am–12noon and 2–6.30pm) and on Saturday until noon.

Museums

Most state-run museums are closed on Monday or Tuesday and between noon and 2pm. There are no fixed opening times for smaller museums. Ask at the *Syndicat d'Initiative* or *Office de Tourisme*.

A slice of Normandy

Postal services

Stamps *(timbres)* are available from post offices, tobacconists *(tabac)* and bars which sell cigarettes *(bar-tabac)*. There is one tariff for letters and postcards which amounts to approximately 50 cents.

Souvenirs

The best souvenirs from Normandy can be either eaten or drunk. If the journey home is not too long, then some fresh cheese from one of the weekly markets makes a welcome present. A bottle of Calvados will survive the journey home more easily and is sure to be well received.

Clothes sizes

Check the children's clothes sizes

Most shops will let you try on clothes *(essayer)* before buying. Children's sizes, in particular, tend to be small compared with UK and US age ranges. Hypermarkets have good-value children's clothes.

Public holidays

New Year's Day, Easter Monday, 1 May (Labour Day), 8 May (VE Day), Ascension Day, Whit Monday, 14 July (Bastille Day), 15 August (Assumption of the Virgin Mary), 1 November (All Saints), 11 November (Armistice Day 1918), 25 December (Christmas Day). Small food shops and souvenir shops, however, often remain open on these days.

Telephone

Have a card handy

More card-operated telephones *(télécartes)* are likely to be found than the old coin-operated models. Post offices and *tabacs* sell the plastic cards with 50 or 120 units. Local calls cost around 20 cents with a *télécarte* for three minutes. The cheap tariff for long-distance calls applies on weekdays from 7pm to 8am, Saturday from 2pm to 8am on Monday and on public holidays. The cheap rate for calls abroad are at the same time.

All numbers in France consist of 10 digits and do not require another code when calling from one *département* to another. Omit the 0 when calling from abroad.

To make an international call, dial 19, wait for the tone to change, then dial the country code, followed by the area code (omitting any initial 0) and the number. AT&T, tel: 19-0011; MCI, tel: 19-0019; Sprint, tel: 19-0087.

Time

French time is one hour ahead of Greenwich Mean Time, six hours ahead of Eastern Standard Time.

Voltage

Apart from one or two exceptions where 110V is still used, mains voltage is 220V. It is worth buying an adapter for continental sockets if you are intending to take any electrical appliances.

One hour ahead

Medical

Visitors to France can expect to have to pay for medical treatment, should it be necessary. Although travellers from EU countries are advised to acquire the E111 certificate, which entitles holders to take advantage of health facilities in other EU countries, in practice not all doctors will accept it, preferring to make private arrangements with patients. It is therefore much safer to take out ordinary travel insurance which generally meets the full extent of any claim. Information is available from travel agents and health insurance companies.

For minor ailments it is often worth consulting a pharmacy (*pharmacie*, easily recognisable by its green cross sign). Pharmacies have wider 'prescribing' powers than chemists in the UK or US. Emergency opening times for pharmacies are usually published in the local newspapers, sometimes in the tourist offices (*Syndicat d'Initiative or Office de Tourisme*) but are always on display on the pharmacy door.

In cases of medical emergency, either dial 15 for an ambulance or call the Service d'Aide Médicale d'Urgence (SAMU) which exists in most large towns and cities – numbers are given at the front of telephone directories.

Emergencies

Ambulance: tel: 15
Police: tel: 17.
Fire *(sapeurs-pompiers)*: tel: 18

The disabled

A list of accommodation which is suitable for the disabled can be obtained from the A.P.F., Délégation de Paris, 22 rue du Père-Guérin, F-75013 Paris.

Newspapers

Newspapers can be bought at kiosks, bookshops or in *bar-tabacs*. There are some regional newspapers such as *Paris-Normandie*, *Ouest-France* or *Presse de la Manche*. Foreign newspapers are available from good newsagents and bookshops.

Read all about it

Accommodation

The choice varies from a historic castle or luxury hotel to private rooms in a farmhouse. Most hotels are accredited by the *Direction du Tourisme* and there are five different categories. Hotels which have been approved by the tourist office can be identified by the hexagonal blue plate showing the letter 'H' at the entrance. The number of stars on the plate indicates the degree of comfort and also the price range.

In this guide, the first three categories are shown under the heading €€€, €€ and € in descending order of expense. A number of hotels, holiday homes and private rooms are not approved by the local tourist board and hence are not classified. A list of all hotels in the region can be obtained from the following address: Comité Régional de Tourisme de Normandie, 14 rue Charles Corbeau, F-27000 Evreux, tel: 02 32 33 79 00, fax: 02 32 31 19 04.

Castles and stately homes
There is wide choice available to those who wish to spend the night in opulent surroundings. Converted castles and former stately homes are usually to be found some way off the beaten track.

Relais et Châteaux, 9 avenue Marceau, F-75116 Paris, tel: 01 47 23 41 42, fax: 01 47 23 38 99; www.relais-chateaux.com In the UK: 35–37 Grosvenor Gardens, London SW1W 0BS.

Good Value
In recent years, more and more good-value accommodation has become available throughout France. New, reasonably-priced hotels are springing up everywhere. Most are to be found outside large towns and close to the motorway network, making them ideal for breaking a journey with an overnight stop. For good standard accommodation with en-suite facilities, you can expect to pay as little as €25 per night for a family room for three.

The Grand Hotel, Cabourg

The main chains that offer this are: Akena, Balladins, Etap, Fasthotel, Ibis, Marmotte, Formule 1, Mister Bed, Onestar Plus, Première Classe, Villages Hotels. (Brochures for these are usually available from the French Tourist Office). Campanile Hotels (tel: 01 64 62 46 46; www.campanile.fr) are worth looking out for, these two -star establishments, part of the Envergure chain of hotels, are particularly proud of their good value restaurants offering home-cooking with menus starting at around €15.

For reservations call: **Formule 1**, tel: 08 36 68 56 85; **Accor**, tel: 08 92 68 56 85; www.hotelformule1.com; **Ibis**, tel: 08 92 68 66 86; www.ibishotel.com; **Etap**, tel: 08 36 68 89 00; www.etaphotel.com.

Logis de France

The hotels in this group with its distinctive symbol of a yellow fireplace on a green background are usually smaller, family-run concerns, mainly located in country areas. Logis de France Service, 83 avenue d'Italie, 75013 Paris, central reservation, tel: 01 45 84 83 84, fax: 01 44 24 08 74; www.logis-de-france.fr

Relais du Silence

Expect to find these hotels in delightful, peaceful surroundings. The hoteliers are committed to providing high quality regional dishes.

Secretariat Relais du Silence, 2 passage du Guesclin, 75015 Paris, tel: 01 44 49 90 00, fax: 01 44 49 79 01; www.silencehotel.com

Holiday homes

Gîtes Ruraux are holiday houses or flats, usually set in the country. The organisation of the same name monitors the quality of the accommodation. UK booking office: 178 Piccadilly, London W1V 9DB, tel: 020-7493 3480. The Fédération Nationale des Gîtes de France is at 9 rue Lazare, 75009 Paris, tel: 01 49 70 75 75, fax: 01 42 81 28 53; www.gites-de-france.fr

Chambres d'Hotes

101

CHAMBRE D'HÔTES

Chambres d'Hôtes are private houses which provide simple and cheap overnight accommodation similar to English 'Bed and Breakfast'. The standard of the accommodation is graded with stars (from * to ***).

Ferme-auberges

These privately-run inns can be found all over Normandy and most offer overnight accommodation. Their menus will usually contain regional specialities and locally-produced drinks. Many of these establishments belong to the Gîtes de France organisation (*see above*).

Youth hostels and camping

A full list of youth hostels in Normandy can be obtained from your local Youth Hostel Association. An international youth hostel card should be obtained before departure. There are two different organisations in France:

Fédération Unie des Auberges de Jeunesse, 27 rue Pajol, 75018 Paris, tel: 01 44 89 87 27, fax: 01 44 89 87 10/49; www.fuaj.org. *Ligue Française pour les Auberges de la Jeunesse*, 67 rue Vergniaud, 75013 Paris, tel: 01 44 16 78 78; www.auberges-de-jeunesse.com

In addition, there are international centres run by the Union de Rencontres Internationales de France, 27 rue de Turbigo, 75002 Paris; www.ucrif.asso.fr These hostels are affiliated to the one or other of the youth hostel organisations.

Book your space in advance

Camping and caravans

During the high season advance booking on official sites is recommended. A full list of camp sites in the region is available at all tourist offices. Alternatively, Michelin publish an annual guide to camp and caravan sites.

Fine dining in the Relais des Gourmets

The Holiday Inn

Bayeux

€€€ **Grand Hôtel du Luxembourg**, 25 rue Bouchers, tel: 02 31 92 00 04, fax: 02 31 92 54 26. Comfortable hotel in central location; **Lion d'Or**, 71 rue St-Jean, tel: 02 31 92 06 90, fax: 02 31 22 15 64. Luxury town-centre hotel in historic 18th century building.

€€ **Churchill**, 14-16 rue St-Jean, tel: 02 31 21 31 80, fax: 02 31 21 41 66. Good terms for half board, in two lovely old buildings linked around a courtyard.

Caen

€€€ **Dauphin**, 29 rue Gémare, tel: 02 31 86 22 26, fax: 02 31 86 35 14. Set in a former 18th century priory, this pleasing hotel also has a modern annexe. Individual style décor in the bedrooms; **Holiday Inn Hotel**, 4 Place Foch, tel: 02 31 27 57 57, fax: 02 31 27 57 58. On the southern side of the city near the racetrack.

€€ **Moderne**, 116 Bld Maréchal Leclerc, tel: 02 31 86 04 23, fax: 02 31 85 37 93. Post-war hotel with clean and pleasant rooms. Wonderful views over the roofs of Caen.

Cherbourg

€€€ **Hôtel Mercure**, Gare Maritime, tel: 02 33 44 01 11, fax: 02 33 44 51 00. Opposite ferry terminal. Modern and functional hotel.

€ **Moderna**, 28 rue Marine, tel: 02 33 43 05 30, fax: 33 43 97 37. Small hotel in central location with colour scheme reminiscent of *Les Parapluies de Cherbourg* (the famous film *The Umbrellas of Cherbourg*).

Dieppe

€€€ **Aguado**, 30 boulevard de Verdun, tel: 02 35 84 27 00, fax: 02 35 06 17 61. A comfortable hotel near the beach; of the sea.

€€–€€€ **Europe**, 63 Bld Verdun, tel: 02 32 90 19 19, fax: 02 32 90 19 00. Overlooking the Channel (Manche), this contemporary style hotel has a light and bright feel about it.

Deauville

€€€ **Libertel Yacht Club**, 2 rue Breney, tel: 02 31 87 30 00, fax: 02 31 87 05 80. A recent addition to the Deauville scene with a choice between rooms facing the quay and yachts or the tranquil gardens. Excellent breakfasts – but no restaurant.

€€ **Continental**, 1 rue Désiré le Hoc, tel: 02 31 88 21 06, fax: 02 31 98 93 67. Late 19th century building located close to the railway station. The rooms are a little small but have good double-glazing and are comfortable.

Évreux

€€€ **Mercure**, Boulevard de Normandie, tel: 02 32 38 77 77, fax: 02 32 39 04 53. Évreux's finest hotel, contemporary architecture.
€€ **France**, 29 rue St Thomas, tel: 02 32 39 09 25. Central, yet quiet location. Traditional and pleasant hotel.; **L'Orme**, 13 rue des Lombards, tel: 02 32 39 34 12, fax: 02 32 33 62 48. Good location in the centre of town.

Le Havre

€€€ **Hôtel de Bordeaux**, 147 rue L. Brindeau, tel: 02 35 22 69 44, fax: 02 35 42 09 27. All of the town centre sights are within easy walking distance; **Mercure**, Chaussée G. Pompidou, tel: 02 35 19 50 50, fax: 02 35 19 50 99. A fine hotel, probably the best equipped in the city; **Vent d'Ouest**, 4 rue Caligny, tel: 02 35 42 50 69, fax: 02 35 42 58 00. Recently renovated hotel with bedrooms decorated according to different themes. *Montagne*, *Campagne* and, of course, *Mer*, all feature.
€€ **Hôtel Marly**, 121 rue de Paris, tel: 02 35 41 72 48, fax: 02 35 21 50 45. An elegant hotel between the port and cultural centre.
€ **Celtic**, 106 rue Voltaire, tel: 02 35 42 39 77, fax: 02 35 21 67 75. This rustic hotel is small and welcoming. No restaurant.

Honfleur

€€–€€€ **L'Écrin**, 19 rue E. Boudin, tel: 02 31 14 43 45, fax: 02 31 89 24 41. In the old town of Honfleur, this elegant 18th century hotel is a treasure-trove. Old French and Norman style, littered with antiques, is blended with Far Eastern high standards of welcome and service.

Mont St-Michel

€€€ **Digue**, tel: 02 33 60 14 02, fax: 02 33 60 37 59. Situated on the mainland not far from the causeway on the main approach road to the island (D976)
€€–€€€ **Hôtel du Mouton Blanc**, Intra Muros, tel: 02 33 60 14 08. Lovely sea views from this pleasing timber and stone building.

Rouen

€€€ **Mercure-Champ de Mars**, avenue Aristide-Briand, tel: 02 35 52 42 32, fax: 02 35 08 15 06. A very clean 3-star hotel only a short distance from St-Maclou church. Bedrooms recently renovated.

Hôtel Normandy, Evreux

103

Index